COMMON SENSE ABOUT INDIA

COMMON SENSE ABOUT
INDIA

by

K. M. PANIKKAR

NEW YORK

THE MACMILLAN COMPANY

1960

© K. M. Panikkar 1960

First Printing

Printed in the United States of America

Library of Congress catalog card number: 60-15047

CONTENTS

CONTENTS

INTRODUCTION

THIS WORK SEEKS to present a picture of new
India, against the background of the national movement and the general revival of her political and social
life.

The most significant feature of India's nationalism
is the attempt to create a synthesis between the old and
the new. In every aspect of her new life can be seen the
influence of Western thinking, mainly due to the
active association with Britain covering a period of a
hundred and fifty years and to the revolutionary
changes that took place in Europe during the twentieth
century. The objective of the Indian national movement, at least after Mahatma Gandhi assumed its
leadership, was not limited to the achievement of
political independence. Gradually it evolved a programme which included the modernization of India's
social institutions and the creation of economic and
political conditions which would enable her to attain,
in time, the standards of the most progressive countries
of the world. What India has sought to do during the
last twelve years is to give effect to this programme.

And yet, what India is seeking to achieve is not
Westernization of her life: she seeks reform of her
own institutions, not a replacement of them by institutions developed in Europe and borrowed indiscrimin-
ately, without reference to her own needs. More
properly, her aims can be described as a response to

the challenge of Western ideas. Whether it is in relation
to caste and untouchability, or to the joint family and
the closed village life, Western thought has acted as a
catalyst, enabling India to find her own solutions
rather than to borrow the solutions which the Western
countries have worked out for themselves. The free
acceptance of such ideas and their assimilation in the
national tradition are characteristics which differentiate
Indian nationalism from the nationalism of most other
Asian countries. This is in the genuine spirit of Indian
tradition, which has, in all the great periods of Indian
history, freely borrowed and assimilated knowledge and
ideas from others.

The two essential characteristics of modern India,
which are shaping its future, are its attitude to the
doctrine of change and its approach to the new sciences.
Indian society, at least during the last thousand years,
has, broadly speaking, been static. It believed that, as
society was based on immutable laws, to bring about
changes in social organization, unless they were meant
to re-establish what was assumed to have been the ideal
conditions of the past, was something bad and therefore
to be resisted. During the period of Muslim authority
beginning with the thirteenth century, Hindu society
was on the defensive, and consequently greater importance was attached to the maintenance of old forms, and
to an unreasoning loyalty to inherited traditions.
Moreover, Islam itself believed in an unchanging
society organized according to the injunctions of the
Koran. Even during the early period of British
authority, such revolutionary thinkers as Ram Mohan

Roy, who sought to make radical changes in Hindu social structure, based their reforms on an appeal to ancient scriptures, thereby claiming that what they sought to do was to restore the purity of Hinduism rather than to introduce innovations.

The emphasis on the necessity for continuously re-shaping society to meet changing conditions is entirely modern, and results mainly from the advancement of scientific thought and the economic revolutions brought about by the application of science to society. It was only in the first decade of the century that this doctrine of change began to gain ground in India. Its wide-spread acceptance is one of the central facts of the Indian situation today. There is no aspect of society which independent India has not sought to change.

A second direct outcome of India's prolonged contact with the West is her attitude towards science. The most important development in India in the post-independence period is the determination which she has shown in catching up with the scientific advances of the West, and in utilizing the new scientific knowledge to the solution of her own problems. She has realized from the beginning that no permanent progress can be achieved by a country on the basis of borrowed or second-hand science; that unless a country is capable of independent research in basic scientific problems, and further possesses a considerable body of scientific personnel capable of utilizing the latest knowledge for productive purposes, she will always lag behind others in the race for progress. This approach to modern sciences is what places India in a category by herself among the newly independent states of Asia. The chapters that follow seek mainly to describe how India is giving practical shape to these ideas ; how an ancient society, which had remained static and wedded to institutions, customs and ideas unsuited to the modern world, is trying to adjust herself, and to build up a new life for her people.

But there is a further aspect of India's development which, though important, is not dealt with in any detail in this book. Apart from her acceptance of the doctrine of change and her approach to modern sciences, the most important result of British rule in India is the change it has brought about in her conception of defence. As a result of her geographical position, India was never in the past aware of the modifications in warfare and strategy which brought about far-reaching changes in the world. Till the twelfth century, no foreign invasion ever penetrated beyond the Punjab. Even the Aryan penetration broke down on the Sutlej. The great kings of Persia extended their domain only to the Indus Valley. Alexander's army only reached halfway up the Punjab. Though Kushans, the Huns and other foreign invaders no doubt established transient kingdoms in the Punjab, and occasionally conducted raids into the interior, the Gangetic Valley and the peninsula had never been subjected to foreign rule till the beginning of the thirteenth century. The reason for the sudden collapse of the Indian kingdoms in northern India was that India continued to depend on trained elephants and half-trained infantry, while major revolutions were taking place in warfare of which she was ignorant. Again, though the people of India had been hardy seafarers, and had not only navigated the Arabian Sea and the Bay of Bengal but sailed out into the Pacific, establishing colonies in distant lands, they had at no time acquired an appreciation of sea-power. When Vasco da Gama arrived on the west coast of India, with guns mounted on his ships, something new and unforeseen entered into Indian history. Never previously had sea-power threatened India. Though the Portuguese had neither the strength nor the organization to undertake any conquest of India, the British in due course were able to bring the whole of India under their control as a result of their uncontested mastery of the seas.

India learnt from her association with Britain this basic lesson, that no country could uphold her independence, or indeed live as a progressive nation, without keeping pace with developments in the science of defence. The Indian Army which Britain recruited and trained fought on three continents and gained an enviable reputation. Though recruited and maintained by a foreign power, mainly in its own interests, the organization of the army as inherited by India was a contribution of the greatest importance to free India. It constituted the basis for a national defence force, free from political interests, recruited from all parts of India, and therefore a major force towards India's integration. Again, though the Indian Navy at the time of India's independence was only a small force, Britain had made India realize the supreme importance of the sea for India's defence. Moreover, ever since India became independent, the British Government has continued to assist India to build up her naval forces and enabled her to share in the tradition and experience of the Royal Navy. During the last twelve years, India's achievement in building up a national army, navy and air force is a fact which is of the greatest importance to her development as a free nation.

Except in the border area, the transfer of power from the British Parliament to the Constituent Assembly of India at midnight on the 14th August 1947 was not accompanied by any of the melodrama associated in history with the word "revolution". And yet, looked at from any point, it was indeed a revolution. An era had come to a sudden end. To men and women in the most distant parts of the country, the little things that stood for life had changed. For eighty million people in the Princely States their Rajas had ceased to be *andatas*, or givers of food; tenants suddenly found that landlords had no longer either prestige or power. The untouchables and other classes which had been denied rights in the past, even under the British, realized that a new day had dawned for them. The loyalties which had held society together under the British vanished almost overnight. To disencumber India of the wreckage of Britain's imperial polity, the princes, the feudal talukdars and the zamindars, while upholding the unifying factors like the Army and the civil services which Britain had left behind, required indeed an act of revolutionary statesmanship.

What the leaders of India created out of the conditions

resulting from the withdrawal of British power is what is now important. The ideals which the leaders of the national state set before themselves were : politically, to ensure the freedoms associated with a liberal state, to uphold the rule of law, and to give to every section of the community Hindu, Muslim, Sikh, Christian and Parsi—a sense of national solidarity ; economically, to correct the unbalance of Indian economy through a planned development of India's resources, to create a new technological civilization by the combination of science and industry, and thereby to provide a higher standard of living for all ; and, socially, to invigorate and reorganize the vast and amorphous Hindu society, by injecting into it a new sense of social purpose and by codifying its laws, eradicating its harmful customs and integrating it into a single community. In appearance, this has none of the characteristics of a revolution—expropriation, violence or large-scale liquidation of classes—and yet, viewed as a whole, it is a major revolution through democratic processes, decided upon by the Indian leaders from the beginning of their new life as an independent nation.

CHAPTER I

THE BACKGROUND

ON THE 15th August 1947, India, after 130 years of foreign rule and a much longer period of eclipse, emerged as an indepedent state. The British, who after a hundred years of continuous warfare had become the effective sovereigns of the country, left India, handing over their authority to the people. Opinion outside India was generally sceptical about the ability of the new state to uphold its unity and integrity, and to work a democratic constitution. It was a kind of dogma with most people that India was no more than a geographical term; that the Indian people, with no less than thirteen languages and with large communities of differing historical traditions, could not be considered a nation in any accepted sense of the word; and that such unity as existed was the outcome of a common administration created by the British, which must inevitably break down when the authority of the British was withdrawn. And yet, the outstanding fact of the last twelve years of history has been the integration of India into a single state, exercising undisputed authority from the Himalayas to Cape Comorin.

During the period of British rule, no less than two-fifths of India had continued to be under the sovereignty of Indian princes. Though, in a few instances, like the Nizam of Hyderabad or the

Maharaja of Baroda, they were no more than war lords, taken under the protection of the British, Princely India represented an ancient and continuous tradition of Hindu sovereignty. Over the territories of these princes, Britain had exercised only a right of paramountcy. For the first time in its long history the entire territory was now integrated under a single unchallenged authority, the new Government of India. More, the Government has been able not only to hold together the vast area, provide it with appropriate constitutional and political institutions and effectively maintain law and order, but also to undertake social and economic legislation of a far-reaching character, revolutionizing almost every aspect of Indian life. Clearly, the view that India was but a geographical name with no national unity behind it was superficial, and has been disproved by the history of the last twelve years.

What is it that has enabled India, in spite of many outward divergencies, to belie the prophets of doom and achieve this unity and stability. Basically, it is the unity of the Hindu people. The Hindus who constitute 325 out of the 380 million people of India have been for over 3,500 years a people differentiated from others. The essential beliefs of the Hindu religion, and the social institutions like caste and the family system which marked the Hindus off as a separate people, were in existence long before the time of the Buddha. The domestic ceremonials and rituals which are still widely observed were written down at least three hundred years before Christ. The legal system under

which the Hindus lived was codified more than two
thousand years ago.)

The intellectual unity of the Hindus was provided
by a common classical language, which was purified
samskrita and created in the sixth century B.C. out of
the vulgar speech of the people (*Prakrit*) which to this
day endures without much change and gives a singular
community of thought and expression to the many
regional languages of India. The contribution of
Sanskrit to the preservation of the unity of the
Hindu people and to their continuity in history as
a separate culture cannot be over-emphasized. The
remarkable revival of Sanskrit studies in the nineteenth and twentieth centuries affords striking proof
of the persistence of the Hindus as a separate
people.

Nor is this continuity of the Hindus as a people
evidenced only by their religion, social institutions and
literary traditions. In art, music, dance, and all other
aspects of culture in which a people expresses its
common inheritance, there has been no marked breach
in the traditions of India. The revival of Indian art,
though no doubt influenced by Europe, was on the
basis of India's own traditions. In music and dancing,
Hindu traditions have been practically untouched and
derive almost exclusively from what the Hindus themselves developed long ago. It is therefore an unquestionable fact that the basis of India's national unity
and of her strength as an independent state is the moral
and spiritual unity of the Hindu people.

It must be remembered that, in earlier periods of

Indian history, also, a similar revival of Hinduism pre-
ceded the movements of national liberation. Contrary
to what is generally believed, the Gangetic Valley and
the area to the south of it, including the Deccan, which
constitute the territory of the India of today were never
subjected to invasion or foreign conquest till the end
of the twelfth century. The first real invasion of India
was by the armies of Mohammed Ghori in 1196. It
is true that the Hindu Kingdoms of the Gangetic
Valley fell without effective resistance to his attack
within a decade, and this vast and populous area, at all
times the heart-land of India, was conquered and lay
prostrate before his successor, Kutubuddin. But the
strange fact that is often forgotten is that by the middle
of the fourteenth century the Hindu people of North
India had recovered, and were fighting back the
invaders effectively, while, in South India, a great
national movement, based on a revival of Hindu
religion, had organized itself into the mighty Vijay-
anagar Empire, whose mission was to resist the penetration of Islam into that area. The recovery of Hindus,
even in North India, was such that when Babur
invaded Delhi in 1525 the only effective resistance he
met with came from a Hindu confederacy led by the
Rajput monarch Rana Sanga. Again, when the Mogul
Empire under Aurangazeb began to assert its Islamic
character, it was the Hindu revival under the Mahratta
monarch Sivaji that led to its downfall. Actually, by the
middle of the eighteenth century, authority over practically the whole of Hindustan outside the Punjab had
passed to the Mahrattas. It was only when Arthur

Wellesley (later Duke of Wellington) broke the power
of the Mahratta at Assaye (1803) that the British
became the leading power in India, and only after 1818,
when finally the Mahratta Empire was extinguished,
that the East India Company became the effective
sovereigns of the peninsula.

The prolonged resistance to the British authority led
by the Indian National Congress (founded in 1885)
was also a dominantly Hindu movement, though from
its earlier days it endeavoured to unite all the communities in India under one banner.

There was, however, a significant difference. While
the resistance to Muslim invaders was based on a
revival of orthodoxy, the national movement under the
British was based primarily on a Hindu reformation
and a basic reorganization of Indian life. The resistance
to the Muslims was based on a defensive organization
of Hinduism, on a greater rigidity of Hindu practices,
and was mainly reactionary in character. Such reform
movements within the Hindu religion as the impact of
Islam generated were considered eclectic, if not
heretical. During the British period the situation was
fundamentally different. In this case, Hinduism re-
organized itself to meet the challenge of modern ideas.
As the reformed Hinduism is the basis of India's
national life today, it is necessary to deal with it in a
little more detail.)

In Bengal, when the British authority was first
established, Hinduism which had for five hundred
years been the religion of a subject race was in a state
of extreme depression. Hindu society itself, burdened

by superstitions, strange practices and absurd cults, seemed to be on the point of dissolution. To the Christian missionaries, established at Serampore, then a Danish settlement, this state of affairs appeared to afford an opportunity to embark on a policy of extensive proselytization. Their activities met with some success at the beginning, but they produced a reaction which was of far-reaching consequence. It helped the more educated Hindus to re-examine their beliefs and to undertake a reform of Hinduism to meet this new challenge. Ram Mohan Roy (1772-1833), the leader of this movement, was an exceptional man, who may well be considered the founder of modern India. Though born of a Brahmin family and brought up as a strict Hindu, his education was through Persian which was then the court language. Later, when he entered the British East India Company's service, he learnt English, which opened to him the whole field of Western liberal thought. It was at this period that Ram Mohan Roy came into contact with the missionaries of Serampore, whose attempt to convert him led Ram Mohan to study Hebrew and Greek in order to go to the original source of Christian faith.

His studies led him back to the *Upanishads*, the early Hindu philosophical treatises, and to a new interpretation of Hinduism. The Brahma Samaj which he founded had thus a dual inspiration in the matter of religion, Hindu as well as Christian, but its outlook in social matters was neither Hindu nor Christian but European and derived its ideals from the Enlightenment of the eighteenth century.

The dual character of the Hindu Reformation, religious and social, was thus emphasized from its very beginning. Ram Mohan was an advocate of modern education through English, of the emancipation of women, of the abolition of caste and of legislation for purposes of social reform. The religious reform he initiated had only a limited success, but it was the precursor of other and more significant movements which in the course of a century transformed Hindu religious thought and reorganized Hindu society. The leading figures of this great movement were Shri Ramakrishna, who gave orthodox Hinduism a new vision of religious truth, which his principal disciple, Vivekananda, preached all over India ; and Dayananda, a Gujarati monk who established, principally in the Punjab, a militant sect known as the Arya Samaj, which, claiming the Vedas to be a revelation, preached a strictly monotheistic doctrine, and condemned the institution of caste, worship in temples and the accretions of later Hinduism. The Arya Samaj also undertook missionary work, not only to strengthen the faith, but to re-convert those who had accepted other religions. Mention must be made, too, of Mrs. Annie Besant, for many years President of the Theosophical Society, who brought to the propagation of new Hinduism the methods of European organization and propaganda. The dynamism of the movement has by no means died down. Ramana Maharshi and Sri Aurobindo are but two of the better-known religious personalities of our own times who have contributed to this revival of Hinduism as a modern religion.

The movement for social reform also gained momentum at this time. But, in the absence of a legislative machinery, such institutions as caste, untouchability, pre-puberty marriages, etc., could not be eliminated. The significant development during this period was the radical change of opinion in regard to these matters, which enabled the government afterwards to tackle them without effective opposition.

Two other factors contributed to this far-reaching internal revolution in Hindu society. The first was the system of education which Britain had introduced in India. In 1835, under the inspiration of the historian, Thomas Babington Macaulay, then Law Member of the Government of India, a basic and far-reaching decision was taken by the East India Company to develop higher education through the English language. Macaulay believed that, once the Indian people became familiar with Western knowledge, Hindu society would dissolve itself. The missionaries who championed this system of education hoped that it would provide them with the opportunity of a massive conversion of Indian intelligentsia. But the results of the new system were quite contrary to the expectation of its authors. The new Macaulayan education was a unique effort made by a powerful government for over a century to educate the upper classes of a society, heirs to a different religion, and social system and to an old civilization, in a foreign language, itself the vehicle and instrument of a dynamic culture. Its beneficient results, in providing an educated leadership, in modernizing Indian languages, in creating the spirit of criticism and

introducing modern sciences to India, deserve the
highest praise. In the modernization of India, this
system of education played a decisive part. But what
it failed to achieve was either the undermining of the
Hindu religion or the dissolution of Hindu society.
On the contrary, as a direct result of this system of
education, it became possible for Hindu society to reform itself on the basis of modern ideas. So far as Hindu
religion was concerned, its effect was to help in a consolidation of thought by providing India with a common language of communication.

The emergence of English as the language of the
educated classes was the second of the two major
factors just mentioned. Its importance as the language
of Hindu reformation deserves to be specially emphasized. In pre-Muslim times, Sanskrit was the common
medium of thought all over India. The great Hindu
Reformation of the eighth and ninth centuries used
that medium. The period of Muslim dominance in
North India limited the use of Sanskrit to professional
scholars and consequently gave rise to the growth of
Indian regional languages. The religious reforms of the
period between the fourteenth and the eighteenth
centuries, like Sikhism, were confined to special language areas. In the nineteenth century, the new education having provided India with a common language of
communication, English, the reform movements
attained an all-India character and consequently took
the form of a national reorganization. It is significant
that all the major works which so fundamentally
changed Hindu thought were written in English. From

the *Precepts of Jesus* of Ram Mohan Roy in the early years of the nineteenth century, to Radhakrishnan's commentaries on the Gita in the middle of the twentieth all the classics of the Hindu reformation, with the sole exception of Dayananda's *Satyartha Prakash*, were written in English. It is in fact the language of Hindu reformation and without it, though the Hindu religion would no doubt have been reformed and society re-organized, the movement would have been regional and the unity of India would have been further broken up.

Two other developments, both resulting from India's association with the West, contributed effectively to the creation of India's unity and the development of a strong national feeling. The first may be termed the discovery of Indian history. India had a considerable historical tradition embodied both in its literature and its semi-religious books known as the *Puranas*, but historical writing was not a part of India's inheritance. Unlike the Greeks and, following them, the Europeans, the Chinese and the Arabs, the Hindu people never developed the art of historical writing. Consequently, at the beginning of the nineteenth century it might have been said with justice that but little was known of the history of the Hindu people before the Muslim invasions. But the patient researches of European scholars gradually opened up to the Hindus the vision of their own past. The first step in this great achievement was the identification of Sandrocottus in Alexander's story with Chandragupta Maurya, the great Emperor whose authority extended practically to the whole of India. After this identification, which provided a key point in history, slowly the story began to unfold itself. The deciphering of the Asokan inscriptions by Princep was the next notable step. From that time, the progress was rapid. Even though the Hindus had produced no history, their emperors and kings had taken care to inscribe in stone the story of their achievements. A systematic survey of inscriptions and epigraphical records was undertaken by the Government of India which provided the basis for an authentic history of the Hindu people up to the invasion of the Muslims. In 1926, R. D. Bannerji, working under the direction of Sir John Marshall, brought to light the Indus Valley civilization, taking the history back to 3000 B.C., and proving that India was a contemporary of Egypt and Sumer and one of the earliest areas of civilization in the world.

Side by side with this, French and Dutch scholars working in Indo-China, Java and the islands of the Pacific revealed to the world the history of Hinduized kingdoms and Indian colonies in those areas. The historical records of the Chinese, meticulously searched by scholars like Pelliot and Sylvain Levy, produced conclusive evidence of the penetration of Indian culture into the Far East. By the first decade of the twentieth century, the achievement of the Hindu people had become—let it be remembered, as a result primarily of the work of European scholars—a source of pride to the Hindus. A new national image came into being, and the Hindus began to see themselves as a people who had not only contributed to the thought of the world, but had in their time been the carriers of civilization and the builders of Empire in far off lands.

Another factor which helped in the growth of national self-confidence was the revival of Sanskrit, and the growth of Indological scholarship, which was again predominantly an achievement of the West. Sanskrit had never ceased to be a subject of study in India ; but it had been confined to the Brahmins, and to certain other classes traditionally devoted to such studies. The philosophical and other works in Sanskrit were, broadly speaking, studied only by a limited class. The interest that the scholars in the West began to take in these subjects, and the publication in English of the great classics of Sanskrit, known only by name to most educated Indians at the time, opened up the treasures of Indian thinking and the masterpieces of Indian literature to the new intelligentsia of India. Mahatma Gandhi has himself confessed that his first knowledge of the *Bhagavad Gita*, the scripture of modern educated India, was through Sir Edwin Arnold's English translation. It would not be an exaggeration to say that it was through the English language that the educated middle class Hindus acquired a pride in their own culture.

The repatriation of the traditions of Buddhism to India was also a part of this process. Buddhism had been practically forgotten in India, and the Buddha himself relegated to the position of a minor deity in Hinduism. Gradually, however, in the second half of the nineteenth century, India re-discovered Buddhism .

through the researches of western scholars. The mass-
iveness of Buddhist philosophy and speculation, and
the achievements of Buddhist teachers in carrying the
message of the Enlightened One to the countries of
the Far East and the contribution of Buddhism to
the literary and artistic traditions of India became
known to the Hindus only by the beginning of the
century. The deep and growing interest of modern
India in what was undoubtedly, till the tenth century,
one of the major factors in Indian civilization also contributed significantly to the national self-image that
new India created for itself.

These major developments affected mainly the
Hindus. The Muslims, who at all times considered
themselves a part of a universal Islamic commonwealth, felt they were the inheritors of the achievements
of the Khalifs of Damascus, Baghdad and Cordova,
rather than successors to the heritage of Hindu India.
The recovery of Indian history before the Muslim
invasion hardly interested them. The artistic glory of
Hindu India, or the growing interest in Hindu thought
and philosophy and Sanskrit literature, contributed but
little to their sense of national pride. The discoveries of
Indian achievements overseas meant nothing to them.
The renaissance of India was therefore something
which the Muslim community, considering themselves
as a ruling race, with their traditions rooted outside
India, looked upon with suspicion more than with
sympathy. When, on the basis of increased self-
confidence on the part of the Hindus, Indian nationalism began to assert itself and ask for political freedom,

the Muslims felt themselves menaced. The foundation
of the Muslim League in 1906, and the demand for
special consideration at the hands of the British—
especially a separate communal electorate for themselves—was the Muslim reaction to the claims of
nationalism.

The Anglo-Muslim alliance forged by the agreement
of 1906 shaped the political future of India. India
became split into two nations, and, though after that
crucial date the two communities co-operated at different times, notably during the Khilafat agitation following the First World War, it was more as allies than as a
single nationalist movement. Besides, from the time at
least of the Tripolitan and Balkan wars, Muslim
politics had become dominated by Pan-Islamic ideas,
though there was also a considerably large body of
nationalist opinion among the Muslims, which visual-
ized India as a single nation-state.

In the period that followed the Great War of 1914-
18, the Indian national movement came under the
leadership of Mahatma Gandhi. The great struggle for
freedom which the Indian people carried on for over
a quarter of a century under his leadership is important
from many points of view. In the first place, it was a
revolutionary mass agitation which carried the message
of national freedom to the villages and enlisted in the
struggle every class in Indian society. Secondly, apart
from its specifically political objective, the Mahatma
gave almost equal emphasis to a radical programme of
social reform, which included the eradication of untouchability among Hindus, the loosening of caste ties

and the acceptance of full equality for women. Thirdly, to Mahatma Gandhi it was the village that was the core of India's life, and its economic and social development was an essential part of his movement.

The prolonged character of the struggle which covered the whole of British India and included all classes of people was itself a matter of supreme importance. It provided India with a tested leadership at all levels, giving her the necessary instruments for implementing national programmes, and, when the time was ripe, for working her democratic institutions. The Mahatma looked upon his followers as a disciplined army (armed solely as he insisted, with "Ahimsa" or non-violence), engaged in a non-violent struggle with a powerful government. The discipline he enforced in the Congress was more than military.

The Congress as an organization was based on elective principles at all levels, and was strictly democratic in its functioning. Working under a rigid discipline and carrying out a comprehensive programme, the experience it gained was of immense value, especially when the struggle extended over a quarter of a century and covered the entire country. In every way the Mahatma was truly the father of the nation.

There were, however, two important aspects to Mahatma Gandhi's personality. As the leader of the national movement he was a fervent believer in Hindu-Muslim unity, a cause for which he laid down his life at the end. His political conceptions were secular, and at no time did he contemplate a Hindu state in India.

But in his personal character he was a Hindu saint, a Mahatma whose life and thoughts reflected the ideal of a *Karma Yogin*, or a saint in action. Much of his activity was devoted to a consolidation of the Hindu people. His insistence on the abolition of untouchability and the total assimilation of these classes in Hinduism; his campaign for the free entry of the untouchables into Hindu temples, which had at all times been denied to them; his historic fast in Poona to prevent the separation of these communities from the body of Hinduism—these constitute clear evidence of the fact that the Mahatma in his own person represented the final phase of the Hindu revival. Also, it must be emphasized that the conceptions on which he based his movement, *Ahimsa*, *Satyagraha*, etc., were directly related to traditional Hindu ideals. The life of extreme austerity which he enforced on himself, and on his personal disciples who lived a communal life with him in his Ashrams (retreats), was also in strict accordance with Hindu traditions.

After the first few years of co-operation on the basis of the Khilafat movement, the Muslim masses gradually withdrew from the national struggle, though a considerable number of forward-looking Muslim leaders continued to share in the direction of national policy. From 1924-25, Hindu-Muslim relations deteriorated, and after 1936 when, under Mr. Jinnah, the Muslim League was revived, a demand began to be formulated for an independent homeland for Islam: in effect, a separation of the Muslim areas and their constitution into a new Islamic state.

A significant development which became noticeable in the 'thirties was the introduction of an economic content into the programme of Indian nationalism. The earlier history of the Congress had no definite economic ideas beyond a vague doctrine that India was being impoverished by foreign rule. Though during the second half of the nineteenth century a considerable textile industry had been developed by Indian capitalists, it was only in the period following the first war that any serious effort was made to breach the walls of British monopoly which controlled banking, insurance, shipping and other major fields of economic life. The growth of Indian capitalist interests turned the attention of some of the younger leaders of the Congress to the economic aspects of Indian freedom. The leader of this group was Jawaharlal Nehru, who, mainly under the influence of socialist thinking, had begun more and more to recognize that the problems of an independent India could only be solved by a comprehensive economic planning. Mahatma Gandhi's own economic vision was that of India made prosperous mainly through village industries. The emphasis during the earlier period of the non-co-operation movement was therefore on the development of village industries and handicrafts. Under Nehru's influence, this gave place to a programme of planned economy. Ten years before India's independence was achieved, when the Congress under the Government of India Act of 1935 took office in 1936, he established a non-official planning committee under the leadership of the Congress, which was the first indication of the economic ideas which had penetrated the younger echelons of Congress leadership.

The growth of the Trade Union movement was also an important development of the inter-war period. Originally organized as a part of the national movement, the trade unions soon became a factor in the industrial life of the country. With the growth of industry between 1919 and 1939, organized labour became a major factor in the development of democratic forces. It must be mentioned that Communist influence also began slowly to penetrate into India. The Russian Revolution had in the early days but little influence on Indian thinking. The efforts of the Comintern in the years between 1921 and 1932 failed almost wholly to have any political impact on India. But, with the growth of the trade union movement and the rise of peasant agitations, Communist infiltration into these fields began to show itself, though generally under the guise of extreme nationalism.

The second great war helped to emphasize these trends, and in 1942, when Mahatma Gandhi decided to launch his last great struggle, known as the "Quit India" movement, it became clear that, after the war, a settlement with Indian nationalism on the basis of independence was the only solution possible. Two difficulties appeared to stand in the way : the demand of the Muslim League for a separate state for the Muslims, and the claim of the Princely States of India to the direct protection of the Crown in England. To Mr. Jinnah and his friends, it seemed obvious that a united India would mean the reduction of 90 million

Muslims to the position of an impotent minority. The only conditions under which the Muslims as a community could have remained equal partners with the Hindus, who constituted nearly three-quarters of the population, would have been if the Princely States had remained as a special interest, and if the untouchables could have been elevated to the position of an independent community separate from the Hindus. This is in effect what the Act of 1935 had sought to do. But Mahatma Gandhi's Poona fast had prevented the separation of the scheduled castes (untouchables) from the main body of Hinduism. Equally, by his fast in Rajkot, he had shown that the interests of the people of the Princely States could not be separated from those of India. Under these conditions, Mr. Jinnah came to the conclusion that in a united India the Muslims would have to be content with the position of a minority. The Muslim League then set out to prove that no political solution which did not provide for a separate Muslim state could be made to work. The communal troubles which started all over India with the great killing in Calcutta were a miniature civil war, which extended from East Bengal to Rawalpindi in the north-west. A partition had become inevitable, and after a few months' experience of a coalition government in 1946-47 the Congress, in spite of its desire to keep the country undivided, realized this. It agreed to the constitution of a separate state, consisting of the indisputably Muslim areas of British India and of such contiguous Princely States as were willing to join.

The secession of the predominantly Muslim areas,

and their constitution into the state of Pakistan, did not, however, affect the historical identity or the cultural tradition of India. It is interesting to recall that when, under the Charter Act of 1832, the Governor-General of Fort William in India was made the Governor-General of India the East India Company's territories extended only up to the Sutlej: the new State's historical identity as India was therefore unquestionable. Moreover while, on the one hand, it is an undeniable fact that the new India was predominantly Hindu, and represented the reformed and revived Hinduism which constituted the strength of the Indian national movement: while it is also important to remember that every area in India considered sacred by the Hindus, from Kamakhya in Assam in the east to Jwala Mukhi in the west, from Kedarnath in the Himalayas to Rameswaram and Cape Comorin in the south, was within the boundaries of the new India, it still contained at the time of partition over thirty-five million Muslims and seven million Christians, apart from other religious sects belonging to the broad Hindu tradition, like the Sikhs and the Jains. The new state could therefore legitimately claim to have inherited the secular as well as the religious tradition of the past, and to be more than Hindustan.

The India which emerged as an independent state on the 15th August 1947 was much more than a Hindu state. The inheritance from the West was in many ways equally important. As we have already seen, the reformation of Hinduism itself was in response to the influence and challenge of the West. The mental background and equipment of the people of India, though largely influenced by the persistence of Indian tradition, had been moulded by over a hundred years of Western education, extending to practically every field of mental activity from social ideals to laws and the political institutions, which, apart from the civil services, were also broadly of Western origin. And so it is true to say that the new India represents a synthesis of the East and the West.

CHAPTER II

TERRITORIAL INTEGRATION AND THE NEW CONSTITUTION

On the 15th of August 1947, India's political geography underwent an immediate and surprising transformation. The Princely States, which constituted over two-fifths of the territory of India, surrendered their sovereignty and acceded to the Indian Union in all matters affecting foreign relations, defence and communications. In the course of another two years they merged completely in the new state, their rulers being content with the retention of their titles and personal privileges and the provision of an ample civil list. Except in the case of Hyderabad, where the Government of India had to resort to a limited police action in view of the chaos into which that state had fallen, this historic and spectacular transformation, which converted India into a nation state, was brought about by peaceful negotiations.

To understand the true significance of this transformation, it is necessary to have some idea of the political geography of India before 1947. The area under the direct rule of Britain (formerly known as British India) was confined to the Indo-Gangetic Valley, the coastal areas and the cotton-growing tracts of Central India, Berar and Nagpur. The vast territories of the interior, extending from the present boundaries of Pakistan, from the south of the Punjab, practically to the Bay of Bengal, were under the rule of Indian Princes. The Nizam of Hyderabad and the Maharajah of Mysore ruled between them over 100,000 square miles in the Deccan tableland, while, in the south, the rich coastal area was under the rule of the Maharajas of Travancore and Cochin. It used to be pointed out as evidence of the divided character of India that the main railway line from Delhi to Bombay, in its direct route of nearly a thousand miles, passed through only 150 miles of British territory.

Nor was this a special feature of British rule. The traditional polity of India from the earliest times was that of an imperial state which, while ruling directly over its own territories, exercised suzerainty and supremacy over its vassal kingdoms. Thus, the Mogul emperors were content to leave the Princes of Rajasthan and Central India unmolested so long as they accepted the suzerainty of Delhi and paid tribute and homage to the Emperor. In fact, some of these princely houses had ruled over their territories for hundreds of years ; the Maharajas of Udaipur were reigning in the region of the Aravalli Mountains at the time of the Muslim invasions. Again, the Maharajas of Cochin had been in possession of their state for a thousand years. While no doubt many of the princes like the Nizam of Hyderabad or the Maharaja of Gwalior were only war-lords with whom the British had made treaties of "subordinate alliance", a much larger number represented the tradition of Indian vassal states which had compromised with every succeeding imperial authority in India.

One common feature of all these states, from Hyderabad and Baroda to the smallest princedom whose
territory covered only a few square miles, was that
their governments were based on princely autocracy,
limited only by the exercise of British paramountcy—
a discretionary but all-embracing right on the part of
the Central Government to interfere in the affairs of
the ruler. A few states like Mysore, Baroda and
Travancore had introduced constitutional reforms of a
limited kind, associating their people with the government. But, broadly speaking, princely rule was autocratic, and no effective political life existed in the states.

It was the doctrine of paramountcy, an indefinable
power—itself arbitrary and autocratic—claimed by the
British government, that held this strange polity
together and gave it the appearance of unity. In the
negotiations of 1946, the British Cabinet declared
officially that paramountcy would cease with the withdrawal of British power, giving the princes false hopes
of an absolute independence. The Chief Minister of a
leading state declared during the period of negotiations
that if Iraq, with only five million people and created
only a few years ago, could be independent and be
admitted to the United Nations, why should it be considered unreasonable that "my state which has a much
larger population and has at least equal resources, and
whose dynasty has ruled over it for at least a thousand
years" should claim to be independent and sovereign.
The court poet of the Nizam, with much less claim,
dedicated a sonnet to the Ruler, addressing him as His
Majesty the King of the Deccan. It was therefore feared

that, with the withdrawal of British power, these Princes, many of whom had quite considerable armed forces, might not submit themselves to the authority of democratic leaders and would prove a stumbling-block to India's effective unification.

When, therefore, on the 15th August 1947—on the day of India's independence—all the Princely States except Hyderabad, Junagadh and Kashmir acceded to the Indian Union, it came as a surprise to most observers. What persuaded the great Princes of India— many of whom claimed to be descended from the sun or the moon, some of whom had ruled over their territories for hundreds of years, and who had all, even in the face of British power, resisted every encroachment on their sovereignty and showed themselves extremely sensitive about the maintenance of their rights and privileges—so suddenly, and without even a token resistance, to agree to give up their sovereignty to the new state? The reasons for this far-reaching revolution, historic yet bloodless, which overnight transformed India from a conglomeration of jurisdictions into a nation state deserve to be analysed. In the first place, once the sense of Indian nationhood developed, the separateness of the states had practically disappeared. The system of education, the integration of economic life, the consolidation of the Hindus as a community— apart from the administrative unity through posts, telegraphs and railways—had created a single Indian people. The states had become mere dynastic interests. As early as 1908, Maharajah Sayaji Rao Gaekwar of Baroda, one of the most notable men of his time in

India and the leading Hindu Prince, emphasized this view in a talk he had with the late Aga Khan. The Gaekwar is reported by the Aga Khan to have said that, as the princes had ceased to represent any but their dynastic interests, independent India should at the first opportunity get rid of them as a possible source of danger to India's unity.

Secondly, the attempt of the British Government in the decade between 1928-38 to separate the Princely States from British India by emphasizing their direct relationship with the Crown had created a growing suspicion in the minds of the people of British India about the intentions of the princes and had weakened greatly the loyalty of the people of the states to their rulers. A powerful States' People's Congress had come into existence under the leadership of Mr. Nehru which not only acted as a counterpoise to the claims of the Princes, but worked for the integration of the states with the rest of India.

In spite of these factors, the peaceful integration of the States with what had been known as British India would not have been possible but for the patriotism and the national spirit of the vast majority of Indian princes, who were prepared to sacrifice their personal dynastic rights to the interests of an independent India. All except a few of the rulers were Hindus; the movement of Hindu renaissance had touched them deeply, in spite of the efforts that the British Indian authorities had consciously made to isolate them. The prospect of an India united, progressive and powerful, for which some of their ancestors had fought in the past, did not leave them unmoved. Besides, the decision to create a separate Homeland for the Muslims (Pakistan) awakened among the Rulers whose states were on the border of Pakistan, especially in Rajputana and the Punjab, the sense of a danger not only to India but to their own states. Though there were a few cases where Hindu princes sought the help of Mr. Jinnah to secure their own independence, the majority of them rallied to India and voluntarily agreed to accede to the new state. Thus, at midnight on the 14th August, when India became independent, all the princes within the boundaries of India—except in Hyderabad, Junagadh, and Kashmir which touched both India and Pakistan had acceded to the Indian Union. The danger of a break-up of India had disappeared.

. The question of integration, however, remained. It was only on the three vital subjects of defence, foreign policy and communications that the states had surrendered their sovereignty when India started her life as an independent state. Obviously this was only a halfway house. By the time the Constitution was ready, India had negotiated with the Princes for the total merger of their territories in the new state. Some, like the states of Orissa and the Mahratta states in Bombay, were absorbed into existing provinces. Others were joined together to constitute new provinces. Only Hyderabad and Mysore continued in their old territorial formation, but, in their case also, the sovereign power of the rulers was taken away and the constitutional structure brought into line with the rest of India. The titles, dignities and immunities of the Rulers were maintained and satisfactory financial arrangements were concluded with them. Thus, with the promulgation of the Indian Constitution in 1950, the traditional structure of India, with a large number of hereditary princes in control of outlying areas under a suzerain power, a system which had endured for over two thousand years, had vanished into a memory.

The importance of this change could not be overrated. India emerged, for the first time, as a unified nation state, with its authority unchallenged from the Himalayas to Cape Comorin. Though she had by the partition lost the areas which constituted Pakistan, a larger area had come under her direct control. The India that emerged was greater in extent and larger in population than the India that Britain had directly administered. Apart from this, the incorporation of the Princely States by abolishing separate jurisdiction, artificial boundaries and conflicting rights made possible the economic growth of India, the planning of her development on a unified basis, the evolution of a common social life—in other words, the emergence of an integrated India.

Though the Princely States had merged with the former British Indian provinces in 1951, it was recognized that the territorial redistribution then effected was only temporary and provisional. The new units created by putting together the former Princely States had in most cases neither sufficient resources nor a suitable administrative machinery. Also, the former British Indian provinces were in many cases artificial units which conformed to no principle and had grown up as a result of historical accidents. Thus the old presidency of Madras consisted of three distinct linguistic groups which stood in the way of a healthy political life. In 1954, therefore, the central government took in hand the question of reorganizing the state-structure of India, and reconstituted the units of the Federation on a rational basis. The two most important aspects of this reform were, first, the disappearance of the units constituted exclusively of the former Princely States, by integrating them with neighbouring provinces or parts of provinces, and, secondly, the reorganization of the provinces themselves. Thus, by 1956, barely nine years after the independence, India was able to rebuild her territorial structure on rational lines, and, broadly speaking, to give to the politics of the country a firm local foundation.

The constitution which emerged from the deliberations of the Constituent Assembly was federal in character, based on a division of powers between the central government and the provinces (officially designated as states) The central government was vested with exclusive powers, not only in respect of defence, foreign policy, railways, air, post, telegraphs and other forms of all-India communication, currency, criminal law and similar matters normally reserved to the centre in a federal constitution, but also with concurrent power over a wide range of subjects where the constituent units are entitled to legislate, subject to the over-riding authority of the centre. The states had authority in matters like land revenue, forests, irrigation, education, industries (except those declared to be of national interest by parliament), municipal and local administration, police and the enforcement of law and order, in fact in matters directly connected with the life of the people. But, unlike most other federations, the Indian constitution not only vested in the central government the residual powers in regard to subjects not enumerated in the constitution, but provided exceptional authority to the central government in a number of ways. Two such powers deserve special mention. The central government, acting through the President, has the power, in the event of a breakdown of administration or in the case of a crisis, to supersede the state government and to have it administered directly through its own agent. Secondly, a special provision is expressly made in the constitution that the executive authority of the states should be so used as not to impinge on or interfere with the authority of the central government.

Briefly it may be said that the Indian federation is heavily weighted in favour of the central government. The purpose which the Founding Fathers had in view was not only to hold in check the fissiparous tendencies which had led to the disruption of former empires, and to maintain the unity which had been achieved after so much struggle, but to endow the central government with all powers necessary in the political and economic field to enable India to undertake a policy of planned development which would raise her to the position of a modern nation, unhampered by the statutory rights of state governments.

The constitution, in its political features, follows

broadly the British Parliamentary system at the centre and in the provinces. The executive authority of the State, though vested nominally in the President, and in the case of the states in the Governors, is exercised by a cabinet, under a Prime Minister, which is responsible to Parliament. At the centre, and in some of the states, the legislature is bi-cameral, the lower house, known as the Lok Sabha or the House of the People (and Vidhan Sabha, Legislative Assembly, in the states) being elected directly on the basis of adult franchise. The upper house at the centre (Rajya Sabha or the House of the States) is constituted on the basis of indirect election from the State Assemblies.

One principal feature of the Indian constitution is that it embodies the gains of the social revolution of the previous hundred years. A Declaration of Fundamental Rights, in two parts, the first enforceable through the courts, and the second described as the Directive Principles of State Policy, which, "though not enforceable by any court are fundamental in the governance of the country", is an essential part of the constitution. The first part emphasizes the principle of equality on which the new Indian State was to be based. It provides that the State shall not discriminate against any citizen on the ground of religion, race, caste or sex. This is expressly meant to cover access to shops, hotels and restaurants, to the use of wells, tanks, roads and other public places. The purpose of this provision is to prohibit the disabilities and social restrictions which previously existed as a result of caste and untouchability, in order to give substance and authority to the doctrine of equality so far as the depressed communities are concerned. Freedom of speech, of association and of the practice and propagation of religion and other normal rights of a citizen in a liberal state are provided for and legally guaranteed, mainly in order to ensure the continuance of the liberal traditions which became a part of Indian political life during the period of British rule. They are also meant as a protection to the racial and religious minorities of India.

The constitution also provides for a Supreme Court entrusted with the duty of upholding the constitution, and, especially, enforcing respect for fundamental rights. During the last twelve years, the Supreme Court has shown itself a vigilant and effective protector of the rights provided under the constitution, especially the guarantees provided to the minorities (for example, the right of the Anglo-Indian community to maintain special schools has been vigorously upheld by the Supreme Court whenever State legislation has tended to encroach upon it).

"The co-existence of several nations under the same State is a test as well as the best security for its freedom. It is also one of the chief instruments of its civilization", delcared Lord Acton. He elaborated the same conception when he added "If we take the establishment of liberty for the realization of duties to be the end of civil society, we must conclude that those states are substantially the most perfect which include various distinct nationalities without oppressing them." The circumstances of Indian historical evolution gave the Indian people a choice of ways. With a predominantly

Hindu population, nearly seventy-five per cent of the total, it was open to India to declare herself a Hindu state, as Pakistan had proclaimed herself an Islamic state. Nor was such an idea without considerable support in India itself. The assassination of Mahatma Gandhi (30th January 1948) by a fanatical advocate of a Hindu counterpart to Pakistan awakened India to the dangers of this choice. The alternative which Indian leaders chose was that of a composite secular state, where each racial, religious minority was given equal rights, guaranteed under law. Discrimination on the basis of religion, caste or race was expressly prohibited. In the India of today, with a population of over 380 million, forty million are Muslims. Christians number seven million, and the Sikhs, though belonging to the general body of the Hindu community, constitute a religious minority of six million. In addition, there are over a million Buddhists, a hundred thousand Parsis, and a few thousand Jews. There is also, spread all over India a tribal population of about twenty million. Under the Indian constitution, all these enjoy equal rights and equal opportunities. Such distinctions as are provided in the constitution are meant to afford protection to certain backward communities like the tribal peoples, for whose welfare and education the State has the obligation to make special provision. It may be claimed with justice that India, though a nation state, has by its constitution endeavoured not only to create a state based on equality and social justice, but to provide every safeguard for minority groups against domination by the majority.

CHAPTER III

DEMOCRACY AT WORK

EARLY IN 1952, India conducted her first general election for both the central parliament and the state legislatures. The electorate was based on adult franchise and numbered over 180 million—that is, as much as the total combined population of the United Kingdom, France, Federal Germany, Belgium, Holland and the Scandinavian states. Over 100 million voters exercised their franchise; over 10,000 candidates contested the elections and over three thousand were elected to man the new democratic institutions that the constitution had set up. Four major parties took part in the election: The Congress, the Praja Socialists, the Communists and the Hindu Mahasabha. It was the greatest experiment in democratic elections conducted openly in the full view of observers from many countries. All the leading public personalities toured the country in the weeks preceding the election and the issues were clearly stated. An economic programme, the first five-year plan, was placed before the country for its approval. Mr. Nehru, as the leader of the Congress Party, had publicly declared that if his party was returned to power, he intended to go forward with a programme of social legislation altering the very structure of Hindu society. The issues had therefore been fairly joined. The country knew what it was voting for. Though the issues were explosive, for the Congress had already passed legislation abolishing large-scale landholding, had declared that it intended to limit the sphere of private enterprise, and had made no secret of its financial policy involving heavy sacrifices by the richer classes, the elections went off smoothly everywhere with no untoward incidents and in an atmosphere of peace.

In 1957 the results were even more striking. The electorate numbered 190 million. The parties were even more clearly differentiated. The programmes were even less ambiguous. The Congress party had been in power in the centre, and in every state except one. Its record in the economic, political and social spheres was for the country to judge. During this period of five years, the Congress party had become progressively more socialist, and had in its convention accepted the creation of a Socialist state as its objective. The Congress was originally a national movement rather than a party. It included all who were for the freedom of India—capitalists, Communists, Socialists, social reactionaries—and had generally the allegiance of the masses. During the Second World War, the Communists had become allies of the British Government after Russia's entry into the war, and consequently they had been forced to leave the Congress. After the war, the Socialist Party, which had been a powerful group within the Congress, withdrew and organized itself as a separate national party. Thus, at the time of India's independence, the Congress had been transformed more or less into a political party and was no

longer an all-embracing national movement; and yet,
it still continued to be rather amorphous in its political
opinion. But events moved fast. The partition of the
country was opposed by the more orthodox Hindus and
the right-wing Hindu opinion slowly dissociated itself
from the Congress and organized itself into a new party
known as the Jan Sangh, which was allied to the older
Hindu Mahasabha. An internal crisis in the Congress
in 1950 led to a further crystallization of the party's
programme. That crisis, which may be considered a
turning-point in the political history of India after
independence, arose out of an open and direct challenge
to Mr. Nehru's leadership. In the election to the Presidency of the Congress party convention, the candidate
recommended by Mr. Nehru was rejected and, instead,
Mr. Purushothamdas Tandon was elected by a
majority. Mr. Tandon, though a respected political
figure, represented in many ways the point of view
directly opposed to that for which Mr. Nehru stood.
He was for a pure Hindu nationalism, eschewing even
the use of leather; he championed cow-protection and
many other obscurantist doctrines. Mr. Nehru, knowing full well that not only the country but the All
India Congress Committee was behind him, answered
this challenge to his leadership by resigning from the
Working Committee of the Congress. This was what
Mr. Nehru called a shock treatment. Mr. Tandon,
recognizing the temper of the country, resigned
and Mr. Nehru himself took over the Presidency
of the Congress, a position which he held for
four years, after which, on his recommendation,

Mr. U. N. Dhebar was elected by the Congress as its President.

This crisis was also a struggle for power within the Congress, between Sardar Vallabhbhai Patel, then Deputy Prime Minister, and Mr. Nehru. Patel was the idol of the more conservative elements in the country. In the party organization, his authority was overwhelming. As Home Minister and Deputy Prime Minister, he had been responsible for the successful integration of the states and for the maintenance of law and order in the country. Though he was no Hindu communalist, his attitude towards the Muslims in India was in some ways opposed to that of Mr. Nehru. In his approach to economic problems and social reforms, also, he was distinctly conservative. In fact, Mr. Patel had no revolutionary urge and was content to let India evolve under a system of nineteenth-century *laissez faire*. To him, with the achievement of independence, the revolution was over. To Mr. Nehru, the revolution had only begun and the crisis which led to the election of Mr. Tandon was merely a reflection of this conflict.

This crisis was thus of primary importance in so far as the policy that Mr. Nehru stood for—a secular state in India in which Muslims, Christians, Sikhs, Parsis and other minorities had equal rights; rapid and planned industrialization; the modernization of Hindu law, and the establishment of what he then spoke of as the "welfare State"—came to be accepted as the official policy of the Congress. Before the general election took place, there was a further split in the Congress as a

fairly large section of the party thought that the leadership was not moving rapidly enough to the left. This
dissident group established the Kisan (Peasants)
Mazdoor (workers) Praja (People) Party, which, after
the elections, merged with the Socialists. Thus, with
the secession of these splinter groups, the Congress
faced the first general election as a united organization
with a definite programme.

The internal conflicts in the Congress had however
not been finally solved by these developments. The
Congress was the inheritor of two traditions, both
revolutionary, but one of which was associated with
certain aspects of Mahatma Gandhi's philosophy and
the other with the political and economic thought of
Nehru. In the eyes of the masses, it was the great
organization that Gandhiji had built up, the great and
unique instrument which had achieved independence
for India. Mahatma Gandhi was a believer in simple
life, in handicraft economy, in the importance of village
life to the future development of India, and was,
generally speaking, against large-scale industrialization.
Mr. Nehru, on the other hand, was a Socialist, who
believed in a balanced but rapid industrialization, one
who wanted Hindu society modernized to suit the
conditions of today. It is characteristic of the Mahatma
that, knowing these differences, he should have nomin-
ated Pandit Nehru as his successor to the leadership of
the country, realizing perhaps that, whatever his
personal views, India was firmly set on the road of
modernization. The contradiction, though not wholly
eliminated, has become less important now. The

Congress at the Avadi session in 1954 firmly declared that its objective was the establishment of a socialistic pattern of society. In the annual conventions of 1955 and 1956, this doctrine has been shorn of its ambiguities and the party as a whole has now been committed to an economic policy directed and largely financed by State investment, the object of which is not only to establish a modern economic structure and provide for a higher standard of living but to eliminate as far as possible the gross inequalities of income. The second five-year plan, effective from 1956, gave meaning and content to this policy. The community projects which are to cover the entire country by 1960 are its programme in relation to rural life. By the time of the second general election, it may well be claimed that the Congress had become a political party—an instrument of government—in the normal sense.

Like all political parties that have enjoyed uninterrupted political power for a long time, the Congress has also developed certain weaknesses which have increasingly come to light during the last few years. A sense of complacency has overtaken the rank and file. A belief in the historic right of the party to govern the country has led to the growth of an intolerance of opposition, of a feeling that it is almost unpatriotic to differ from the Congress. In fact, the Congress has not yet had the experience of being in the opposition. A more significant weakness which, though not new, has come into prominence during the last three years has been the obstruction of what may be called intermediate leadership to the policies of the party. This was manifested most clearly in the matter of land reforms. The leaders of the party in most of the provinces have followed a policy of silent resistance to directives from the central office, and, last year, when it was decided to proceed with a scheme of radical reforms in respect of land holding, it was noticed that, though the party convention approved the proposals, after full discussion, by an overwhelming majority, many leaders in the provinces, some even holding office, were not prepared to carry the policy into effect. The conflict between the older leadership and the more progressive sections of the Congress could no longer be concealed. The election of Mrs. Indira Gandhi to the Presidency of the Congress is, in this connection, a most significant step, as she represents the more radical views of the younger generation. Mrs. Gandhi is the fourth woman to be elected President of the Congress. Her main political activities in the past were connected with the organization of youth for national service (Bharat Seva Sangh) and the creation of a body of radical opinion inside the Congress. Though one of the youngest Presidents of the Congress (she is under forty), Mrs. Gandhi has travelled widely, not only in Western Europe but in the Soviet Union and in China. Her election represents the change-over from the older generation. It is also an affirmation of India's determination to go ahead with the policy of modernization, of resistance to tendencies of social reaction from which the rank and file of the Congress has never been exempt. Educated in Switzerland and Oxford, and alive to the social urges of modern times, Mrs. Gandhi represents a vigorous radicalism in social matters which is of great importance to the future of India.

The party in opposition nearest to the Congress is the P.S.P. or the Praja (People's) Socialists. For a long time there was a socialist group in the Congress led by Pandit Nehru. In 1946, this group, with Jai Prakash Narayan at its head, decided to organize itself as an independent national party. It started however with a handicap. Pandit Nehru held the view that Socialism can best be achieved in India by converting the Congress to that point of view by gradual stages, by a process of trial and error, rather than by organizing a separate party with a rigid ideology. The majority of the Socialist group decided otherwise and left the Congress, which was not weakened in any great measure by this secession. What the Socialists hoped was that the Congress, because of its unwieldy character and amorphous views would, as the governing party, become more and more reactionary and consequently they, the Socialists, would become the inheritors of the progressive traditions of the Congress. As we have seen already, this was not what happened. On the other hand, the Congress policy veered to Socialism, leaving the Socialist Party with no separate programme of its own.

Another source of weakness for the Socialist Party was that, following the traditions of the Labour Party in England, it tried to base its strength on industrial workers and the trade union movement. Here also the alertness of the Congress party foiled this plan. From the beginning of the trade union movement in the period following the First War, the Congress had been closely associated with the organization of labour. After independence, the Congress went further and organized under its own auspices the Indian National Trade Union Congress (I.N.T.U.C.) which was able to retain the allegiance of a considerable section of workers. The Labour portfolio in the Congress cabinet at the centre was held by a leader with trade union sympathies, and the official policy of the Congress was to promote the gradual participation of workers in industrial management. Thus, between the Communists who had the allegiance of the left-wing groups among the workers and the Congress which was able to retain the loyalty of a considerable section, the Socialist Party found itself baulked in every way.

So far as the peasantry was concerned, here also the Socialists had no special programme to offer. The Congress policy of land reform, cautious as it was, kept the peasants fairly contented. Besides, the Planning Commission was actively promoting, through community projects and national extension services, a vast scheme of rural welfare. The Socialist Party was thus driven towards a policy of barren criticism combined with desperate attempts to gain popular support by taking up local grievances, or trying to concentrate attention on issues like Goa.

More important than the Socialists, both because of their organizational strength and the appeal of their ideology, are the Communists. As a group, the Communists have worked in India from the early 'twenties.

They tried, ineffectively, to penetrate the national movement, and their influence till the beginning of the war, generally speaking, was slight. It was the Second World War that gave them the opportunity to build up their strength. After the Soviets came into the war the Communist Party came out as the champions of the anti-Fascist struggle, and offered to co-operate with the British Government in India. The Government was at that time in a very difficult position. The Japanese had reached the borders of India. Both in respect of the Middle Eastern campaign and in the war against Japan, India was Britain's main base. But in the face of the unrelenting opposition of the Congress which had started the "Quit India" movement, and the absence of co-operation from the general public, the wholehearted support that the Communists offered seemed to be a God-send. An unnatural alliance was thus forged by which the Communists became the main instruments for controlling labour agitation and generally for pro-war propaganda. Though it was a *damnosa hereditas*—the charge of having sold Indian nationalism at a time of crisis—from which the Communists have not yet fully recovered, it afforded them valuable opportunity for building up their influence among the workers in industry and generally of strengthening party organization. The end of the war therefore found them better organized and with a greater sense of confidence than ever before.

When India became independent, the Party found itself in a very difficult position. For a time the leadership believed that large-scale political chaos would

follow, and that the Leninist doctrine of revolution-
making could be practised according to text-books.
This was a period of attempts to disrupt communications, to seduce the loyalty of the security forces, and
to sabotage industrial effort. The doctrine preached was
that Nehru was the agent of British capitalism and an
instrument of imperial policy; that the independence
of India was only nominal, and that it was for the Communists to "liberate" the country. The failure of this
policy became evident soon enough. The second phase
was an attempt to establish a Communist base in
Telingana, in the former Princely State of Hyderabad,
and make it a kind of Yenan for the Indian revolution.
But this adventurism also met with disastrous failure.
It was only then that the Communist Party awoke to
the fact that Nehru was no instrument of British
capitalism and that the cry of "liberating India" would
bring them no followers. Also, the Indian constitution
had been proclaimed and a general election on the
basis of adult franchise was soon to take place. The
Communists were faced with a dilemma. They could
either refuse to accept the constitution, and pin their
faith on violent revolution, or contest the elections and
enter central and provincial parliaments. The constitution being democratic, and the parliaments based on
adult franchise, to refuse to participate in the elections
would have been for the Party to write its own death-
warrant. But to go into parliament was also dangerous
for party ideology. Its activities had to be constitutional.
The parliamentary group of the Party, however much
it might oppose legislative measures or criticize the

Government, would have to propose amendments, alternatives, and otherwise take part in constitutional work, all of which would weaken the revolutionary urge of the Party. After much consideration, the Party decided to fight the elections, if possible in alliance with other Left Wing groups. In the state of Travancore-Cochin (now a part of Kerala), in the Andhra districts of the then Madras state, and in the Telingana area of former Hyderabad, the Party did reasonably well and obtained a fair percentage of votes. In the centre, in fact, and in the state of Travancore-Cochin, they became the leading opposition group.

In the elections of 1957, the Congress again won by an overwhelming majority, securing 369 out of a total 494 seats in the centre, and majorities in all provinces except in Kerala, where the Communists, with the support of a few independents sponsored by them, secured a majority and thereby came to power.

Having decided to participate in the functioning of democratic institutions, the Communists did not confine their activity to legislative bodies. Wherever they had sufficient strength, they contested the seats in municipalities, district boards and village councils. In at least one district board they were able to obtain a majority. The town of Alleppey also voted a Communist majority into municipal offices.

The result of all this has been to import a sense of realism into the politics of the Party. In the realm of national policies, they, like the Socialists, found themselves deprived of their main war-cries. India's friendly relations with China and the Soviets, and her neutrality in the Cold War, left the Communists nonplussed. Reluctantly they had to range themselves behind Mr. Nehru and the Congress. The visits of the Soviet and Chinese leaders, and the flow of friendly deputations from the countries of the Soviet bloc, left the Communist Party without a line of attack in their favourite ground. Internally, also, when the success of India's plans was being praised by Chou En-lai and the Soviets were actively co-operating towards the success of the second five-year plan, the Party could not come out to oppose the Congress programme. The elections of 1957 reflected these tendencies.

The other party organizations which may be considered here are the Hindu Mahasabha and the Jan Sangh. The Mahasabha is a fairly old organization meant originally as a counterpoise to the Muslim League. It was frankly communal. Though as a political organization it never counted for much, its influence was by no means negligible, for its views were shared by a very large section of ordinary Congressmen. Immediately after Independence, the Mahasabha suffered a great setback as a result of Mahatma Gandhi's assassination, for its leaders were associated with the militant Rashtriya Swayam Sevak Sangh, who were popularly credited with responsibility for the crime. The Jan Sangh, or the People's Party, whose ideology is similar, gained greatly in consequence, especially as it was able to attract the sympathy of the millions of refugees from West Pakistan. The refugee population was bitterly anti-Muslim, as they had lost everything in Pakistan and had been uprooted from

their homes. In the Punjab and adjacent areas, the
Jan Sangh is a party enjoying considerable popular
support.

There are also other provincial parties, some like the
Gana Tantra Dal of Orissa consisting mainly of dispossessed Rulers and landowners, while others like the
Kerala Revolutionary Socialist Party are to the left and
have a local following.

Till 1959, all major opposition to the Congress on an
all India level had come from the Left. But the forces
of conservatism which, faced with the reforming
fervour of Mr. Nehru and the momentum of the
revolutionary era, had been effectively silenced found
a champion in Mr. C. Rajagopalachari, one of the most
respected figures in Indian public life. In politics he
had been a close associate of Mahatma Gandhi from
the earliest days of the non-co-operation movement.
He retired into private life in 1954 after having been
governor-general, the last to hold that high office, and
later Home Minister in Mr. Nehru's Cabinet. Since
his retirement he had become a relentless critic of many
aspects of Mr. Nehru's domestic policies especially in
matters affecting Hindu social life. In 1959 (June-
July) he put himself at the head of the growing
opposition to the socialist programmes of the Congress
government and organized, with the assistance of leading industrialists and other elements of conservative
opinion, the *Swatantra* party, which emphasized the
virtues of private enterprise in industry and the
necessity to oppose the growth of state power. To
what extent the new party will be able to influence

public opinion in the next elections it is difficult to say.

The organization of all-India parties with definite programmes and policies has greatly helped to make democracy take firm root in India. All the national parties put forward candidates, not only for parliamentary elections but for municipal, district board and village council elections. Consequently, election propaganda and organization, and criticism of public measures are not confined to times of general election, but go on all the time with a view to the control of some town, village or district. Democracy is thus a functioning process in India, and democratic activity is a regular feature of political life throughout the country.

During the first three years of India's independence, it was often forecast that India would go the way of Nationalist China, with the Congress in the role of Kuomintang ; that it would become more and more unrelated to the people and that, unwilling to alienate the big capitalists and the powerful forces of social reaction ever present among the higher castes in India, Congress leadership would lose its revolutionary and democratic urge, thus unconsciously preparing the ground for Communism. This is what the Communists hoped for and the western world feared. Such might have been the development if the first national government had not realized that the essential thing in India was to get the democratic processes to function. The Indian constitution was discussed and passed by the Constituent Assembly within three years. It was a notable achievement. But a constitution by itself could not have warded off the danger implicit in the fate of the Kuomintang. The real foundation of India's democracy lay not in its central and provincial parliaments, but in its broad-based local and municipal organizations, the village councils, the district boards and municipalities, all of which are democratically elected on the basis of adult franchise. Democracy began thus to function at all levels, not merely as a machinery for electing central and provincial parliaments. When the coping-stone of this system was placed in the early part of 1952, it became evident that India had embarked on a career of democratic development for which there was no parallel, at least in Asia.

So far, Indian democracy has shown itself to be a vigorous growth. It has shown notable courage in dealing successfully with difficult and complicated problems like the reorganization of Hindu society by legislation after full public debate, the changing of the economic pattern of India by comprehensive and large-scale planning, and the rearrangement of the territorial structure of the provinces. It has also not hesitated to tax the people for its schemes of development. In fact, Indian democracy has been able to keep up the democratic urge and canalize it.

Where and how did this young democracy receive the moral strength to undertake these tasks? Primarily, it was the prolonged struggle with the British authorities—extending over a period of thirty years—that gave to the Congress its democratic character and its tested and tried leadership. After Mahatma Gandhi took over the direction of the Congress, its organization from top to bottom was based on the elective principle. Membership of the Congress was open to anyone who accepted the Congress creed of freedom for India and was able to pay a nominal annual fee of 4 annas (4 pence). Local committees of the Congress were elected bodies. From out of the provincial Congress committees, the controlling body known as the All-India Congress Committee was elected. The President of the Congress was elected by the vote of the Provincial Committees. These elections were by no means formal affairs. They were hotly contested, and at least on one occasion the Mahatma's own recommendation for the presidency of the Congress was over-ridden by the electorate. Congress politics from 1920 worked as an effective training ground for popular democracy.

Equally important for democracy is the question of national and local leadership. Democracy can function properly only where there is dispersed leadership which is trusted by the people. The national struggle provided India with a political élite, whose patriotism had been tested over decades and whose devotion to public causes had been proved and demonstrated by their personal sacrifices. Not only was India lucky to have a leader who embodied in himself the causes which India held dear—democracy, economic progress, social equality, the rule of law—but she had provided herself with a fairly large body of political workers at all levels, who, by long experience in the national movement, had gained the confidence of the masses. These two factors helped her to develop a steady political life on a democratic basis.

How important this training in leadership in the national movement has been, not only for the Congress but for India as a whole, may be seen from the fact that the top leaders of the opposition parties in the country also had their training in political work in the Congress. The Socialist Party as we noticed before was a section of the Congress which, on ideological grounds, separated from the parent organization. Its leaders are all of them old associates of the Mahatma and Mr. Nehru. Even in the Communist Party, some of the top-ranking men like E. M. S. Nampudiripad, A. K. Gopalan, were active followers of Gandhiji and respected Congress leaders at one time.

Another most important factor which helps India to maintain and strengthen her democratic institutions is the rise of the new classes to power as a result of adult franchise. The Congress was a mass movement with a middle-class leadership. But elections based on adult franchise have brought to the forefront classes which had at no time exercised effective political power in India. This phenomenon we shall deal with elsewhere. But the significant thing to be remembered here is that the first general election itself showed a marked shift of political power to groups which were anxious to prevent a return to the old order. The former untouchable classes, agricultural labourers, small peasants and others elected to the provincial legislatures were aware of their rights and anxious to improve their condition. They know themselves to be the real beneficiaries of democracy.

Democracy has undoubtedly taken root in India, but

it has certain obvious weaknesses, which should not be forgotten. In the first place, there is the fact that a large percentage of the electorate is illiterate. No doubt literacy is no test of political wisdom ; and in this age when, through the radio and the cinema, political education can reach the masses, the mere fact of illiteracy need not be considered as a serious handicap to the functioning of democratic institutions. Nor is it possible to concede that an illiterate peasantry provides greater opportunities for the growth of totalitarianism. Germany under Hitler and the Soviets under Stalin did not suffer from illiteracy. In fact, Germany was among the most advanced nations in the matter of education but that did not prevent the growth of Nazism. All the same, an illiterate democracy is a weakness, because the interest of the voters is more likely to be concerned with local problems which the electorate understands than with national or international problems which it does not understand.

Secondly, there is the perennial question of caste. In India, caste loyalties are strong even where caste has ceased to be an important factor in social life. It is not the four castes, Brahmins, Kshatriyas, Vaisyas and Sudras, that are important in this connection, but the closely-knit smaller groups, known as sub-castes, the members of which live in neighbouring areas and are in close social relationship. They are more like clans, with the same feeling of solidarity. The political power which the electorate enjoys has led at least in the first instance to a strengthening of this group loyalty, though ideological differences of nationally organized parties are challenging it. These group loyalties are exploited by politicians. This is undoubtedly one of the marked weaknesses of Indian democracy today.

Thirdly, there is a wide disparity of economic, political and social conditions in different parts of the country, unavoidable in a population of three hundred and eighty million. Thus a programme which is suited to the conditions of Bombay may not be suitable for Assam, with its large aboriginal population. The variations are sometimes so great that national parties have to adjust their programmes to suit local conditions. For the development of national parties, this is an undoubted necessity, but it constitutes a weakness which cannot be overlooked.

Lastly, there is the greatest weakness of all, the tendency to social reaction which exists among the upper classes of Indian society. For the present, their voice has been silenced by the dominant urge for change, inherited from the period of national struggle and kept alive by a strong leadership believing in social progress. But it would be foolish to overlook the fact that there are groups in India which command the silent loyalty of millions who believe in the sacredness of cows, in the sanctity of old customs, in the veneration to be accorded to Brahmins, in the superiority of things Hindu, and so on. The hold of the past is indeed great on the Indian people, and if there is any weakening of leadership, reaction may take control, which may imperceptibly affect democracy itself.

In view of the startling reversion to authoritarian non-parliamentary types of government in most of the

Afro-Asian countries in the recent past, especially the abrogation of the constitution and establishment of military rule in Pakistan, questions are often asked about the chances of democracy in India. The fear is often expressed that, with the slow rate of industrial progress as compared with China, and the gradual weakening of Congress leadership, India also may turn her back on democracy and either opt for a Communist régime in the hope of a quick and radical settlement of her problems, or surrender to a military dictatorship. In all the questions often posed in the West, such as "After Nehru what?", there is the lurking fear that, once his guiding hand is withdrawn, India may follow the other Afro-Asian states and become either Communist or reactionary and non-democratic.

Democracy in India is not so firmly rooted as to enable us to say that no such danger exists. But, as against its apparent weaknesses, there are also many important considerations which are in favour not only of a survival of democracy but of a rapid growth of democratic forces. The danger from a military dictatorship similar to that which has taken control in Pakistan may first be considered. The Indian defence forces are built up on an All-India basis in which the different ethnical and regional groups are fairly balanced, preventing the growth of an army leadership which could challenge the authority of the civil government. There is no pre-eminence allotted to any group, community or regional area which would enable a military leader to claim loyalty or allegiance to himself. Secondly, the healthy provincial feeling, based on separateness of language, and the federal organization of government, make a coup d'état by a group of politicians or military leaders difficult, if not impossible. It is generally argued by superficial critics that the existence of large language groups and their consolidation into linguistic provinces constitute a serious weakness to the national unity of India, that they represent divisive tendencies which in the past led to the breakdown of the central authority in India. On the other hand, it is obvious that it is the existence of these large linguistic units with a strong sense of identity that is the guarantee of India's democratic structure, for any attempted coup d'état in the centre would be met with the most determined resistance of provincial governments jealous of their rights and of their regional culture. Thirdly, democracy in India is not confined to parliamentary institutions. It functions vigorously, as already explained, at every level, in village organizations, in local government, in powerful popular organizations like the trade unions and the national political parties, and in the Congress itself, which, at least from 1920, has functioned as an elected democratic organization. Its direction is in the hands of an elected president assisted by a Working Committee, in which provincial and group representation is never overlooked. Following the Congress, the other parties, with the exception of the Communists, also have a thoroughly democratic organization. The danger of democratic forces in India yielding to a military dictatorship would not therefore seem to be serious.

The possibility of a Communist take-over in India through constitutional methods also deserves consideration. The Communists are an effective and well organized party in India, and in one of the states, Kerala, they gained political power through normal democratic processes. After the general election of 1957, they became the actual government of the state. But this success, notable as it was, should not lead us to over-estimate their power in the country. In the larger states of India (with a population of over 330 million) the elections showed no great support for Communism. In Uttar Pradesh, with a population of nearly 65 million, the Communists were able to secure only nine seats in the local parliament. In Bihar with a population of 45 million, the Communists polled only five hundred and thirty-seven thousand votes and secured only seven seats. In Madras (where they won only four seats), Madhya Pradesh (two as against 232 won by Congress), Rajasthan (one), Bombay (thirteen against 232 to Congress) and the Punjab (six), they were unable to make any real impression. So, from the all-India point of view, the Communist threat today is insignificant. But the question is, will it remain so? What will happen after ten or fifteen years no one can foresee, but in the immediate future, that is to say, within the next ten years, the challenge of Communism to Indian democracy would seem to be negligible.

It must however be remembered that Communism is a dynamic political doctrine and may well adjust itself to democratic processes as a result of its own internal changes. The characteristics of Communists which offend liberal and democratic sentiments may get transformed, or at least modified, as a result of economic prosperity and the growing sense of security. In any case, it is difficult to prophesy about the prospects of Communism in India without being able to foresee what Communism itself will be like in the next stage of its evolution.

The leadership of democracy in India, which worries Western observers and leads them to ask the question, "What after Nehru?", must now be considered. Democracy, it should be remembered, is not a system of government which postulates a unique leader. In fact, its success is based on dispersed leadership—leadership at all levels. It is true that in times of great crisis, democracy, unless it is able to throw up a leader commanding the confidence of the nation, will face great difficulties. It was India's good fortune that at the time of her emergence as an independent nation she was able to find a leader in whom the entire country could put its trust and who therefore had the authority to guide it in its most difficult days. But even during these days of his unchallenged leadership, Mr. Nehru, though he has symbolized the nation's struggle for independence, as well as its immense effort to maintain and consolidate its independence, has been no Führer, but an essentially democratic leader building up a true democratic structure of government, and working through parliamentary and popular institutions. The question therefore is not whether there will be another Nehru to guide India, but whether India's political institutions are so organized as to be able to select a suitable Prime Minister ; and, further—this is even more important—whether there exists in India a sufficient reservoir of leadership from which to choose a suitable successor.

Apart from the political dangers which every new democratic structure faces from other ideologies, either authoritarian or Communist, there is a more insidious threat which also cannot be overlooked. This is the reduction of democratic institutions to a façade behind which a powerful bureaucracy controls the policies and administers the country under a new system of absolutism. Even well-established democracies in the West are not free from this danger. The late Chief Justice Hewart, in his remarkable work entitled *The New Absolutism*, drew attention to the growth of these trends even in England. It is obvious that this danger is much more serious in India, whose political tradition for over two thousand years has been that of an administering state where the common people at all times identified government with officialdom. Especially under the British rule, a system of undiluted bureaucracy had functioned for over a century, and neither the monarch nor the political leader counted as against the local officer, a doctrine of "Ma-Bapism", of looking upon the official as the "father and mother" of the common man had been encouraged. As this tradition has not been altogether eliminated, the danger of the bureaucracy overshadowing democracy and using the democratic forms only as a cover for arbitrary authority cannot be overlooked.

Also, it is obvious that, in a planned society, the technician and the administrator will acquire new power over highly important spheres of national activity with democratic control becoming more and more formal and ineffective. The immense administrative machinery that India has had to develop, when planning became a major concern of government and large-scale industrial organization came directly under government control, may at first sight appear to generate a threat to India's democratic institutions. The relationship between the administrative services and popular control is one of the most difficult issues of the modern state. How has Indian democracy dealt with this question?

At the beginning stages of India's independence, political leadership, both at the centre and in the provinces, had no doubt to lean heavily on the small corps of trained administrators that the British had left behind them, but the most significant development during the last ten years has been the gradual and unmistakable assertion of parliamentary authority over the administrative machinery. By emphasizing the responsibility of Ministers to Parliament, even in administrative matters, parliamentary democracy has asserted its control over the bureaucracy in a decisive manner. The most recent instance of this healthy development was when one of the most powerful Ministers of the central government resigned, after a judicial enquiry into certain administrative measures which it had been claimed were put into effect under the directions of civil service officials. The rights and wrongs of the issue are unimportant. No doubt the officials concerned acted honestly and in a way they considered desirable in the general interest. It may also be true that the Minister was unaware of the decisions taken. But Parliament placed the political responsibility for these administrative actions on the Minister concerned and he, accepting that constitutional position, resigned.

This case was particularly significant because the issue was publicly argued and decided. Previously also there had been instances where the Indian Parliament had asserted its democratic right to control the administration, but the decision in the Krishnamachari case was the final and decisive affirmation of the supremacy of Parliament and its agents over the administration.

It is not only by the enforcement of parliamentary authority through the Ministers over the civil services that democratic India has ensured that the administration shall not develop into a bureaucratic absolutism. The strength of the Indian bureaucracy was based at all times, and more especially during the British period, on the concentration of authority in the District Officer who represented the *Sirkar* in all its might and majesty to the people. Today, though the position of the District Officer continues to be important, as the chief administrative officer of the area, much of the active work of government, especially where it relates to economic, social and other development, has passed into the hands of non-officials, elected district boards, *janpad* councils, community leaders and other representatives of the public. Also, no longer is the District

Officer the "representative" of his area, as he was under a bureaucracy, when it was his duty to put forward the claims of his district to the higher authorities. Today the elected representative in the local parliament eclipses him in this role.

In fact, the marked tendency has been to depreciate the political importance of the civil servant while strengthening his administrative position. The danger to India's democratic institutions from the growth of a bureaucratic state, cannot consequently be considered serious.

CHAPTER IV

SOCIAL CHANGES

No less important than the political changes is the planned social revolution that the government has initiated in India. What India has attempted during the past ten years is to reorganize the structure of Hinduism, and bring India's social institutions to the level of other modern countries.

Hindu society, from the earliest times, had had three distinguishing characteristics—the caste system with its corollary of a submerged base outside caste, known as untouchables ; the joint family ; and a system of law, which, however much it varied from place to place, had a unity of ideas and conceptions.

The caste system is a very complex social organization, which divided the whole society theoretically into four castes, but in practice into innumerable subcastes within the four-fold division. The division into Brahmins (the priestly or learned class), Kshatriyas (the fighting class), Vaisyas (the traders), and Sudras (the great mass of working people), was at no time more than notional. But even so far as the Brahmins, who constituted the only integrated caste, were concerned they were also, from the very earliest times, engaged in other professions besides learning and priestcraft. Neither was learning in any manner confined to the Brahmins. With the other castes, except for certain domestic rituals, the definitions did not hold at all. Thus the fighting classes were not confined to Kshatriyas. In all historic times, the royal families of India were mostly non-Kshatriyas and included impartially Brahmins, Vaisyas and Sudras. So the broad division into four castes was more theoretical than otherwise. More important sociologically in this system were the innumerable "sub-castes" into which society came to be split up. While everywhere else the symbiotic circle widened with social evolution, in India it became continuously fragmented with the splitting up of the sub-castes into smaller and smaller units.

The joint family was a system under which property was held in common and the brothers and sons lived together under the same roof. Property was inherited by coparcenery, and not by succession. Hindu law, too, was a very complicated system of rights and obligations based on ancient texts and local customs. For various reasons these had never been codified and Hindu society was thus kept together by an archaic system of laws which traditionally came even to be associated with Hindu religion. One aspect of this system of Hindu law was its effect on women. Under the ordinary Hindu law, women had but limited right to property. An independent life for women had never been contemplated under Hindu law and their economic dependence emphasized this at all times.

During the hundred years preceding independence, many causes had helped to weaken the traditional foundations of society in India. Later, under Mahatma Gandhi, the movement for social integration had

become a part of the struggle for freedom. Every aspect
of the Indian revival—the religious reformation, the
political struggle, the change in economic life, the rise
of new classes—all these had their effect on the social
structure. The movement for a reform of religion
helped to show that many of the customs which the
Hindus had considered as part of their religion had no
religious sanction; caste, child marriage, etc., were
seen as social institutions without any relation to religion. The political struggle helped the people to realize
that a society which was being continuously divided
into smaller and smaller groups could not be effective
as a nation, and that a social reorganization was an
essential preliminary to India's nationhood. The change
in economic life, leading to the growth of new cities,
helped in the breakdown of caste restrictions. In this
way, by the time that India achieved her independence,
society was ready for radical changes.

Superficially, in 1947 Indian society presented the
same familiar features as in the past. Over 40 million
people were still considered untouchables. The caste
system seemed unaffected in the main and the reform
movements of the past appeared to have touched only
its outer fringe. Women still suffered from social and
legal disabilities. The joint family, though considerably weakened, was functioning. A casual observer
might well have said that, while India had achieved
political progress, socially she was still living in the
past.

The constitution, as we have already seen, was the
first clear declaration that new India was determined to

bring about a social revolution. In unequivocal terms it abolished untouchability. It proclaimed the equality of women. It laid down as a Directive of Policy that the state should work for social justice and equality.

Accepting all this as an earnest of India's desire for progress, the world was naturally sceptical about the realization of so far-reaching a programme. It seemed easy to abolish untouchability on paper, but how was it to be carried out and put into effect? How could traditions of centuries be transformed in this manner by a declaration of principles? Equally, how was Indian womanhood to achieve independence and freedom when the basic institutions of society, family, marriage, divorce and inheritance rights assumed her dependence? How was the caste system, which had survived all assaults on it from at least the time of the Buddha, to be destroyed? Not only the sceptics abroad, but the orthodox in India argued that all this was no more than the wishful thinking of a few enthusiasts.

But the sceptics have in this case been proved to be wrong. India was ripe for a social revolution, and battles already won in the public mind had only to be given legislative shape and form. By a series of measures, discussed and debated in public for over 8 years, the Indian Parliament re-organized the social structure of Hinduism. Marriage law was unified all over India, abolishing by a single Act of Parliament not only the numerous forms of customary marriages, but changing the basis of orthodox Hindu law itself. The new marriage law is contractual, permits marriages between different castes, sanctions divorce and is monogamous.

Each one of these is directly contrary to the principles on which Hindu law was based. Though the practice among many communities within the Hindu fold was different, the theory of Hindu law was that all marriage was sacramental, witnessed by the sacred fire, binding the parties to a permanent and indissoluble union. The new law repudiates this doctrine totally. The permission of marriages between different castes is even more far-reaching in its importance than its contractual form. Neither Hindu law nor custom permitted inter-caste marriages, though it was not irregular for a man of a higher to marry a woman of a lower caste. The strength of the system of exclusive castes lay in this prohibition. It was the foundation on which that mighty system had been erected. The new law legalizing inter-caste marriage strikes at the very root of the inherited social organization of the Hindus. It is the most effective single action taken so far to abolish the caste system.

The law provides for monogamy and permits divorce under certain conditions. Though polygamy was never widely prevalent in India and was not socially favoured except among the Princes and the higher nobility, Hindu law permitted more than one wife—and in certain cases, such as barrenness or even the failure on the part of the wife to give birth to a son, it was considered proper to have a second wife. The insistence on monogamous marriages is therefore an important change.

It is not only by the new marriage law that the position of women in India's new society has been radically changed. The inheritance law has also been changed, enabling women to become financially less dependent on men. Daughters have been given an equal right to inherit with sons, and the old doctrine of women enjoying only limited rights in regard to property has been discarded. The breakdown of the joint family system has also helped to give women a new dignity.

The legislative measures which have broken down the system of caste also deserve consideration. The right of civil marriage, as we have noticed, struck at the legal basis of caste. The idea that some castes were superior had legal sanction in the marriage of the Hindus till 1955. The *pratiloma* marriage, the marriage of a higher caste woman to a man belonging to the lower caste, was, according to all conceptions of Hindu law, illegal and void. The new law makes no such distinction between superior and inferior castes, and marriages between Hindus of different castes are of equal validity.

Legislation with regard to the control of Hindu religious endowments has also had a direct effect in weakening the hold of caste. Formerly, the lands belonging to the temples, monastic institutions and similar bodies were under the exclusive control of the Brahmins, or the priestly caste. Today, in many parts of India, they have been placed by legislation under trustees elected without reference to caste. Thus, for example, in the State of Madras, the Religious Endowment Board, which looks after the administration of temple properties, consists mainly of persons who do not belong to what are known as the higher castes.

The abolition of landlordism has also helped to weaken the hold of caste. One of the main sources of strength of the Brahmins was the support they received from the princes and nobles who traditionally considered it a part of their function to provide for Brahmins in order to gain spiritual merit. The annexation of the Princely States, followed soon after by the abolition of large-scale landlordism, affected the prestige and authority of the Brahmins who were left without this powerful support. It may well be said that independent India has by indirect methods achieved a revolution, the full effects of which are beginning to be appreciated only now.

It is in the treatment of the problem of untouchability that New India has shown the greatest courage. The problem of untouchability was something special. It was a system under which large classes of people, numbering altogether over forty million, had been denied elementary social rights, such as the use of public wells, and were treated as less than human beings. In the extreme south of India, this oppression was carried to such lengths that even the shadow of an untouchable was supposed to pollute a higher caste man. Though in most of the provinces of what was known as British India the more inhuman restrictions, such as the ban on the use of public transport and the denial of admission to public schools, had generally speaking, disappeared, in the territories of most of the Indian Princes these oppressive customs held sway till the day of India's independence. But even in the provinces of "British India", the untouchables suffered

from numerous disabilities, they were forced to reside
in special areas outside the village and were generally
speaking confined to menial and degrading occupa-
tions.

Mahatma Gandhi had put the abolition of untouchability in the forefront of his political programme. By
choice he lived in untouchable colonies, and in his own
ashram he had members of the community as inmates.
So, when the Constituent Assembly met, one of the
resolutions it passed was that untouchability should
forthwith be abolished. The constitution of India gave
effect to this resolution and directed Parliament to
enact legislation defining offences arising out of this
practice and to prescribe suitable penalties for them.
The Untouchability Offences Act came into force all
over India on the 1st of June 1955. The intention of
the Act is to make illegal the enforcement of any dis-
ability against persons formerly belonging to the untouchable classes. Under this Act, every person is free
to enter any place of public worship which is open to
other persons professing the same religion. He may
bathe in and use waters of any stream, tank or well to
the extent used by others. Any person obstructing such
uses may be punished under the Act.

Obstruction of access to shops, public restaurants,
hotels, places of entertainment and similar facilities is
also an offence when it is directed against a member of
these classes. In actual practice, it was in these two
categories that the grievances of the untouchables were
most serious. Whereas, formerly, they were not
admitted to Hindu temples, nor allowed to use the

same wells, to bathe in the same tanks, to enter restaurants, hotels, etc. and were in many parts of India
excluded from places of public entertainment, under
the new Act, not only have these rights been expressly
extended to members of the former untouchable communities, but it has been provided that when such a
denial or prohibition is attempted in the case of an
untouchable, the law shall presume that the commission of the forbidden act was on the ground of
untouchability.

To encourage the practice of untouchability and to
take part in any boycott or excommunication are also
offences under this law. It will be seen that untouchability can have no place in India, so far as law can
ensure it.

If it were merely a question of law, this age-long
custom, against which the reforming zeal of great men
from the Buddha to the Mahatma has fought, might
still have continued, at least in different forms, and in
inaccessible rural areas. What has made it impossible
for untouchability to survive in any shape anywhere
has been the working of democratic institutions. Adult
franchise has entrusted these classes with the power to
vote. The constitution further provides for special
representation of untouchable classes in Parliament and
in local legislatures for a limited period. As the system
of local and village organizations in India is also based
on adult franchise, these backward communities have
awakened to the power that has been given to them,
and even in remote villages they do not hesitate to use it
to establish their rights. The political parties which

contest the elections, even at the lowest level, appear as champions of the rights of the backward classes, whose votes generally determine the results.

Also, both because of their voting strength and the ideological tradition inherited from Mahatma Gandhi, members of these classes are included in central and provincial cabinets. One of the most powerful members of the central cabinet during the last twelve years, Mr. Jagjivan Ram, the Minister of Railways, was once considered an untouchable. In every province, members of these classes hold important portfolios. In Parliament they play an important part. The enjoyment of actual political power and the consciousness of voting strength and, more than all, the social and political awakening which independence has brought with it have given reality to the law, which otherwise might well have been a dead letter.

There are numerous other factors which have helped to bring about the social revolution which in many ways is the most important development in modern India. The Community Projects, which now cover more than 300,000 villages, have helped to create a new life in the rural areas of India, upsetting rapidly the inherited social structure of the past. The static quality of Indian village life was the main source of India's old weakness —the backwardness of women, the stratification of social classes based on status and the practice of untouchability. In the areas under the Community Projects these customs have undergone rapid change. The leadership in the rural movement has gone to new classes, and to a large extent it is shared by women.

The social revolution in the villages is organized, given shape and continued by this movement.

‒ A second factor of importance is the growth of new industrial towns. Formerly, cities had grown up gradually in centres which had a political or religious significance. Consequently, to a large extent, they tended to reproduce the social structure of the country. Only with industrialization did urban life begin seriously to affect the social structure of the community. But even in Calcutta and Bombay, which were major industrial centres, orthodoxy had continued to exist, with communities voluntarily living apart and reproducing the social traditions of the areas from which they had originally arrived in the city. In the new industrial towns, planned after independence, the situation is totally different. They have no political or religious background. The township is built around certain major industries and the workers, recruited from all castes, live in "colonies" built for them by the industrial concerns. Thus, in Chittaranjan, where the great locomotive works are situated, around which a new township has grown, the social planning did not take into consideration the question of caste or the regional peculiarities of the new population. The rapid process of India's industrialization has resulted in the creation of numerous townships of this nature, and the sociological effects of planned towns on a traditional society like that of the Hindus have been mainly to weaken the hold of custom, caste, food taboos and similar characteristics of Hindu life.

—The great influx of the refugee population is yet

another thing that has helped to reorganize social life in large areas. As a result of partition, over nine million refugees have reached India from Pakistan. Out of these, nearly six million, from West Pakistan, had been totally uprooted and came to India leaving their all behind. A further three million came from East Bengal. Misfortune of this kind is a great equaliser, and the traditional divisions of society were forgotten in the great calamity that overtook them. The refugee population from West Pakistan has been settled and rehabilitated in India, a truly gigantic task, which strained the capacity of the Indian Government to the extreme. But what is of importance here is the social reaction of this immense movement of people. Distributed all over North India, they contributed largely to the creation of a new society. The new townships which they helped to build were in themselves sociological experiments of great significance. The townships of Nilokheri and Faridabad—both of which are now centres of considerable industrial activity, built by the refugees themselves with Government advice and assistance—mirror the new social life of India.

Finally, the functioning of India's democratic institutions has brought about a marked shift in social balance. Broadly speaking, political power has shifted from the urban professional classes and the rural landowners, who produced the leadership in the past, to new people, who had no great voice in public affairs before. This is most noticeable in the states. In Rajasthan, for example, where political power as well as social prestige had for a long time been concentrated in the Rajput community, today the Rajputs have not even a single representative in the Cabinet. The Jat cultivators, on the other hand, who in former days had only limited rights on the land they cultivated for the Rajputs, have become a most important group in the legislature. In Madras, for long considered the centre of orthodoxy and the citadel of Brahmin power, the Ministry does not contain a single Brahmin member. The Chief Minister comes from a caste which was considered untouchable. Agricultural communities like the Padiyachis, who had been considered as belonging to the lower castes, suddenly felt themselves important, through acquisition of political power. In fact, everywhere in the provinces the emergence of "new people" has been a notable feature in the political development of the last twelve years.

This rise of the new people is a major social revolution, the significance of which is but little realized outside. At every period of Indian history, the life of the nation has been continued and kept alive during periods of crisis by some unknown group erupting on to the stage of history. Instances are the Mahrattas, a previously unknown peasant people, in the seventeenth century; the Jats, a community of peasants in North India, in the eighteenth century; the new middle classes, recruited without reference to caste or social conditions and formed as a result of Western education, in the nineteenth century—all new peoples. What differentiates the new movement from these earlier instances is that it is not confined to any area but is nation-wide, and has political, economic and social motivations. It is in fact a major social revolution which brings to the forefront classes and communities which in the past contributed but little to national life. The intellectual and political life of India in the past drew its strength only from a small minority. Today, what may be considered the most important fact in India's life is the release of the energies and intellectual potential of the vast masses of the people. This can be seen in every aspect of India's life. The literature of the regional languages in the past was the monopoly of the higher classes. Today this is no longer the case. In the economic field, again, the trade union movement was originally organized under the leadership of middle-class intellectuals. Today, broadly speaking, it has been taken over by the working classes themselves. The tribal people, numbering over twenty million, confined for over two thousand years to their mountain fast-nesses, have begun to take an active interest in social and public life. Thus, the general social picture of India has, within the last twelve years, changed almost beyond recognition as a result of a planned and directed revolution. The India of today is no longer a socially backward country dominated by caste and anachronistic customs, with millions of people denied social rights. The survivals of these things may be seen everywhere, but society is moving fast towards an integration of a magnitude and significance which entitle it to be called a major revolution.

CHAPTER V

ECONOMIC CHANGES

THE POVERTY OF India had become proverbial. At the time of India's independence, the most disturbing fact, which provided the greatest challenge to her leadership, was the fact that the vast majority of her people lived at starvation level. Indian economy was not only backward but was incapable of providing the necessary resources for the betterment of her life, for the provision of education and medical facilities, not to speak of a general rise in the standard of living. With the population increasing at the rate of five million a year, and handicapped by a primitive system of agriculture, India seemed at the time of her independence to provide a convincing example of the truth of Malthus' gloomy prophesies. Her industrial development during the British period was partial and unbalanced, while her natural resources had not been even fully surveyed. New India, if she was to survive as an independent state, had to face these problems, each one of them difficult enough to strain the capacity of a well-established state, but collectively overwhelming in size and complexity.

Nor was this the only difficulty. The partition of the country had left both India and Pakistan with a terrible heritage. Nearly six million refugees, uprooted from West Pakistan, had to be absorbed and rehabilitated in India. Economic life in the border provinces was disorganized in a manner which had not been forseen. The great jute industry of Bengal, for instance, discovered that while all the factories were in India, raw jute came mainly from Pakistan. Also, in the political field, the conflict over Kashmir, another outcome of the partition, led to a diversion of energy and resources. After the first few months of what looked from outside like a drift into chaos, the country recovered rapidly both its administrative and political stability. India demonstrated both the strength of her internal integration and the wisdom of her political leadership when, in the face of these extraordinary difficulties, she was able by the end of 1949 to absorb the Princely States, to promulgate a constitution and undertake a nation-wide general election.

The governing fact in India, which overshadowed everything else at the very start of her independence, was the widening gap between her population and her food supply. During the period of British rule, this problem had not attracted much attention. In 1936, Burma, which was a surplus area in rice-production, was separated from India; with the creation of Pakistan, the major irrigated areas in the Punjab went to that state. Already the Bengal famine of 1942 had demonstrated that, without a regular supply of rice from Burma, India would have to face a large deficit in what was the staple food of over two-thirds of the population. With the separation of Pakistan which was mainly a wheat-growing area, the problem became accentuated. With the population steadily increasing at the average rate of five million a year, the essential issue, on the successful solution of which everything else depended, was to provide food for the people of India. It was only after essential necessities had been provided that new India could think of raising her admittedly low standard of life. It was thus clear from the beginning that, if India were to safeguard her freedom and develop as a progressive nation, everything had to be subordinated to the problem of food production.

The solution of the food problem involved many complicated issues, such as the modernization of agriculture, the provision of perennial irrigation in a country which had been dependent in the past mainly on the vagaries of the monsoon, the reclamation of land that had become uneconomic, and a radical reform of the system of land-holding. Not only economic factors were involved in this question. The conservative and almost static character of the peasantry, living in tradition-bound villages and normally allergic to change, had to be rapidly reformed if Indian agriculture was to be modernized. A social revolution was necessary to make the rural economy of India progressive. In fact, this question touched almost every aspect of India's national life. The stupendous nature of this problem may be recognized from a few simple figures. In 1947, of the 700 million acres which comprise the territory of India, only 220 million were actually under crops. As much as 90 million acres were shown as cultivable waste, other than fallow. Another 40 million were left uncultivated in alternate years.

An equally significant fact was the low productivity

of the land. In respect of all staple crops, India's production per acre is even now much below that of most
countries. In respect of rice, while the yield in Japan
was 4,293·7 lb. per acre, in India it was in 1950 no
more than 1,140·5. In respect of wheat, while the yield
in France was as much as 1,818·06, in India it was only
639·86. Maize and barley showed a similar difference.
It was obvious that, with a reasonable increase in
productivity, India's food problem in relation to her
growing population and her requirements for increased
consumption could be met. But such a result could only
be achieved by far-reaching reforms. The leaders of
India realized from the beginning this essential fact,
and the policy of comprehensive planning on which they
embarked was a consequence of this realization.

The first five-year plan (1951-56) in its economic
aspect concentrated mainly on agriculture. Its industrial objectives were limited : the establishment of a
major fertilizer plant (producing over 350,000 tons of
chemical fertilizers) ; the construction of railway locomotives and wagons, for the purpose of improving
communications and of relieving the pressure on her
foreign exchange ; and such other necessary under-
takings as were related to the problem of increasing her
agricultural production. The main emphasis was on
great irrigation works, hydro-electric projects, meant
to bring under cultivation large areas of land, to control
devastating floods, to make India less dependent on a
variable monsoon and to provide her with power. The
Damodar Valley scheme in Bihar, the Bhakra-Nangal
in the Punjab, the Hirakud in Orissa, the Chambal in

Madhya Pradesh and Rajasthan, and the Tungaghadra in Andhra are but the most important of the many multi-purpose schemes undertaken by the Government of India as a part of the first five-year plan. Sixteen and a half million additional acres were brought under irrigation as a result of the projects undertaken in that period, and under the second five-year plan, which will be completed in 1961, the total irrigated area in the country will reach the figure of 88 million acres.

Though these large-scale and imposing achievements have greatly relieved the situation, they have by no means solved the problem of India's food supply. Apart from the all-important factor of the increase in population, there are other factors which stand in the way of India's immediate success in dealing with this problem. They relate to the uneconomic system of landholding, to the primitive agricultural methods in the villages and to the rigidity of India's social conditions. A semi-feudal landlordism was the feature of land tenure in the rich Gangetic Valley which was under direct British administration. In the Princely States of North India and in Hyderabad a system of *Jagirdari* prevailed, under which the *thakurs*, or nobles, though enjoying no proprietary rights themselves, collected the revenue and exercised feudal authority over tenants and cultivators, whose own rights to the land they cultivated were of the meagrest kind. In the rest of India, where a system of peasant proprietorship, known as *ryotwari*, prevailed, the fragmentization of holdings had become a major evil, preventing any improvement in agricultural methods. Everywhere the superior land-owners had taken to the habit of leasing and sub-leasing their lands, which led a land revenue commission appointed by the British Indian Government to describe this large class of rentiers as "an incubus on the working agricultural population which finds no justification in the perform-ance of material services so far as agricultural improve-ments are concerned, and fails to provide an effective means for the development of the resources of the land".[1]

The reform of land tenure was therefore a problem of great urgency, not only from the political point of view, but from the necessity of increasing agricultural production. But in this matter the Government of India proceeded with undue caution. The first five-year plan recommended to the state governments a moderate programme which included the abolition of intermediaries between the state and the tillers (land-lords, jagirdars and similar tenure holders), security of tenure for cultivators, fair rents, and a right of purchase for the tenants. These were elaborated later during the second five-year plan, so as to include the fixation of a ceiling on land holdings, and the co-operative organization of agriculture, with the ultimate object of village management. Unfortunately, the only effective reform carried out so far has been the abolition of the intermediaries, in itself a radical change, but hardly touching the heart of the problem of food-production. No doubt other measures meant to improve the conditions of the peasantry, such as the fixation of maximum rents and security of tenure, have

[1] Quoted in Gyan Chand, *Problem of Population*, on p. 16.

been enforced in many states, but, broadly speaking, the legislation on land reforms has been directed more towards the emancipation of tenants than to the object of increasing agricultural production.

The elimination of the intermediaries, especially in the prevailing conditions of India, could not by itself lead to an increase in agricultural production. The holdings in most cases are much too small. The peasant is, generally speaking, conservative and educationally backward. In the circumstances, the elimination of large-scale landholding was important more as a social reform than as a step in the improvement of agriculture. Though the Government of India recognized this, the federal structure of the Indian constitution, under which agriculture was a provincial subject, rendered it difficult for them to follow up the reform in land tenure with effective programmes of agricultural development, by enforcing a system of co-operative methods in cultivation or the introduction on any large scale of modern techniques. This became a part of the Government's policy only by the beginning of 1959 when, at Nagpur, the Congress decided by an overwhelming majority to press forward with the large-scale introduction of co-operative methods in farming, thus eliminating alike the evils of the fragmentization of holdings and outmoded techniques of cultivation.

A programme transforming the villages in India in preparation for a far-reaching reorganization of rural life was, however, a part of the first five-year plan. Known as the Community Project and National

Extension Services, this was a comprehensive plan which, in many ways, is the most revolutionary scheme of development undertaken by the Government of India since independence. A Community Project is an integrated scheme of development for a group of about a hundred villages. The National Extension Service is a preliminary stage where the development is not so intensive, but prepares the areas for greater development under the planned system of Community Projects. The underlying idea of both these plans is to create larger rural units provided with modern facilities for economic and social development. They seek to break down the old conservative system of village units, too small for economic planning or community life. Under this system, each project area has a programme of development which, apart from such items as better communications, adult education, sanitation, provision of amenities, includes invariably the introduction of new techniques in agriculture and the encouragement of co-operative societies. The importance of the Community Projects in the programme of rural transformation will be dealt with later. In the context of the problem of food-production, its significance lies in the emphasis it places on getting the new techniques down to the level of the village, and in eliminating the traditional, self-contained, conservative leadership in agriculture and peasant economy.

The unofficial movement of *Bhoodan* and *Gramdan* which is associated with Vinoba Bhave is also in many respects an important activity, meant to awaken the villagers to the social and moral purposes of land owning. Vinoba, though practically unknown in the political field at the time of Mahatma Gandhi's death, was one of his immediate disciples in social work. A meagre and emaciated person, wedded to a life of austerity, he represented the Gandhian tradition in its religious and social aspects. His economic philosophy was then primitive. He believed in self-contained villages, disapproved of large scale industries and machine production, was an advocate of nature cure, preferred walking tours to travel by trains—in fact he may be said to have represented the more extreme aspects of the Mahatma's ascetic habits. Vinoba had not actively interested himself in politics, but after Mahatma Gandhi's assassination he seems to have felt the call to take upon himself the responsibility of awakening the people to the problem of the landless in India. He started his movement originally in Hyderabad, where, taking advantage of a feudal tenure of land-holding, the Communists had in 1947-48 distributed the land to the peasants and tried to establish a base for action. When, through the intervention of the Indian Army, this "little Yenan" was liquidated, Vinoba Bhave realized that the problem of land had remained unsolved. There he brought about through his influence a satisfactory agreement between the landholders who had been deprived of their land and the peasants to whom it had been distributed. Bhave emphasized the moral problem involved and started on his campaign of "land gifts" from those who had superfluity, meant for distribution among the landless. Soon, however, he realized that the question was not one of distribution of plots of ground to the poor, and the new policy which he initiated was the surrender of the entire village land (*gramdan*) for cultivation by the village as a whole.

Though it could not be said that the village gift (*gramdan*) movement has assumed national proportions, its significance can by no means be underestimated. It has awakened the consciousness of the nation to the land problem as a whole, and, secondly, it has popularized the idea of voluntary effort in co-operative cultivation. Vinoba, in the genuine tradition of Mahatma Gandhi, walks from village to village, preaching his message and making the villagers realize both the moral issue involved and the economic value of co-operative effort in cultivation. In short, what he seeks to achieve through his *gramdan* is a collectivization of farms at the village level through non-violent means.

The first five-year plan (1951-56) marked a notable achievement in increasing food production and in laying the foundation of industrial advance. From 54 million tons, food production increased to 63·5 million, irrigated areas from 51 million acres to 67·8 million; in the industrial section, also, a firm basis was laid for a comprehensive advance in the next plan. The national income (in terms of constant prices) increased by about 18%, while *per capita* income also recorded an increase of 11%. The work of the plan was not solely on the economic plane. Education, advanced scientific and technical training, health, housing, the welfare of backward classes and labour were also included in the expenditure under the plan, so that, at the end of the period, India may be said to have laid the foundations of a modern state.

The objective which India has kept before herself from the beginning, and which was reflected in the first five-year plan, is what is known as a mixed economy, in which, broadly speaking, the basic industries will be owned and developed directly by the State, while the private sector will have a defined sphere where it will be allowed to have free play. This policy was not based on any prejudice against private capital. The Indian authorities realized from the start that Indian capitalism was not sufficiently developed to embark on many important basic industries, without which such economic progress as may be brought about would only be of a secondary character. Steel plants, machine-making industries, heavy chemicals, the development of oil resources, the machine-tool industry and similar projects would have to be developed rapidly if the country as a whole were to achieve a self-developing economy. And this could only be done under State control. But a very large sector of industrial effort has been left for the operation of private capital. During the first plan period (1951-56), the private sector made rapid and notable advances, not only in such well established industries as textiles, cement and sugar, but in creating an automobile industry, and in pharmaceuticals, as well as engineering works, and shipping. Some notable beginnings were also made in the public sector of industrial life during this period. A state machine-tool factory, the construction of telephones

(in which India is now self-sufficient), the development of electronics, ship-building, locomotives and
railway coaches, are some of the most important.

The second five-year plan (1956-61), while continuing to lay emphasis on increasing agricultural production by further irrigation and by the introduction
of new methods, is primarily directed towards the
creation of a self-developing economy. The objectives
of the plan as defined by the Government include an
increase of 25% in the national income, a rapid industrialization, with emphasis on heavy and basic industries,
and an intensive expansion of natural resources (coal,
gas, minerals, etc.), in addition to a parallel advance in
the private sector.

In the public sphere, the targets of the second five-
year plan include a 231% increase in finished steel
production (raising it to 4½ million tons); an increase
of 233% in aluminium, an increase of 600% in the
production of phosphates. The over-all industrial production in both private and public sectors is expected to
go up by over 64%. While in 1951 India produced
machinery worth only 4½ million pounds, in 1958 her
production had multiplied by twelve. By the end of the
second five-year plan, India hopes to reduce considerably her dependence on foreign machinery and capital
goods.

Two other aspects of India's economic planning
deserve to be emphasized. The first is what may be
described in Aristotle's phrase as an attempt to realize
"distributive justice". It is inherent in the federal
character of the state and the developed feeling of

regionalism that India should seek to spread her industrial effort all over the country so that no area feels neglected. During the period of British rule, the early development of the cotton industry was concentrated mainly in Bombay, and jute almost exclusively in Calcutta. Under India's system of planned economy, the development programmes are related to the resource and requirements of each area so that every part of the country shares in the effort. Though heavy industries like steel have to be concentrated in areas where the raw materials exist, and consequently some places like the coal- and iron-bearing area of Bihar, are bound to be more industrialized, it is significant that India's new steel mills are located in three different provinces, Bhilai in Madhya Pradesh, Rourkella in Orissa and Durgapur in Bengal. Again, realizing that Madras and the areas of the south have no high-grade coal, the Government of India has embarked on a vast scheme for the exploitation of lignite, with expert assistance from abroad, in order to provide the south with opportunities of large-scale industrial development.

It is significant to note that, if the production of steel and the development of related industries is concentrated in the eastern states, such important programmes as the production of machine tools, electronics, and the aircraft industry are located in the south.

What India is seeking to do by this policy of planned distribution is to strengthen the process of national integration. The size, differences of cultural development and strong sense of regionalism which give India a continental character make it necessary that her integration should be not merely political, based on the frailties of a constitution, but strengthened by a deep sense of economic interdependence.

An equally important aspect of India's new economy is the emphasis on village and small-scale industries. There are three factors behind this decentralization of certain spheres of industrial development. India recognizes, in the first place, that large-scale industries which must inevitably be situated in urban centres cannot absorb more than 10% of her population (i.e. about 40 million people). The vast majority of the Indian people will continue to live in the countryside, and, if the difference between unindustrialized rural areas and the urban centres were to increase, the situation would become dangerous and explosive. To provide against such a contingency, it is essential that the prosperity which comes through industry should in a measure be shared directly by the rural population. Small-scale industries are therefore important as a means of diminishing the differences in economic level between the urban and rural populations.

Secondly, even now, over eleven and a half million people are employed in small enterprises. They produce over 8% of all India's goods and services. If their techniques are modernized, and they are provided with credit facilities, they could form a prosperous section of the national economy, which would help to stabilize social conditions in rural India.

Thirdly, there is the great and living tradition of Indian handicraft and cottage industries which has so far been able to resist the inroads of machine-made products. The silk and hand-loom cotton cloth industries, which employ over two million weavers and whose produce continues to be increasingly popular, as well as other similar traditional handicrafts, are supported and encouraged, not only as important to India's economic life, but as providing employment for village people. [The aim of the Government of India is thus a planned industrial revolution on a scale never previously attempted within the framework of a democratic structure, providing not only for the growth of industry, but at the same time for the elimination of the miseries which uncontrolled industrialization created in the past, and for the distribution of the wealth created to the nation as a whole.)

The total investment projected under the plan for the second five-year period is no less than 6,000 million pounds, most of which (4,500 million) is to be realized by taxation. The strain is no doubt a heavy one, but the social purpose which the Indian leaders have set themselves, that of reducing inequalities in income and wealth and of ensuring a more even distribution of economic power, enables the government to build up a tax structure which will fulfil this social purpose as well as provide the funds for investment.

The main difficulty that India faced during the crisis of 1958 was not in respect of her internal resources. High industrialization of the kind attempted in India involved large-scale expenditure of foreign currencies for the purchase of capital goods, and, as her own capacity to earn the necessary foreign exchange by exports was limited, she had to depend on external loans and credits. This is a problem for all developing economies, an evidence in fact that the development has reached its most critical stage. Through the co-operation of the more advanced states, U.S.A., Britain, Germany and the U.S.S.R., India has been able to tide over the crisis, and the second five-year plan, which will take her into the ranks of highly industrialized countries, will now be completed successfully by 1961.

CHAPTER VI

SCIENCE AND TECHNOLOGY IN INDIA

DURING THE PERIOD of British rule, India had developed a considerable interest in science. Though the system of education that the British had introduced was broadly humanistic and literary, and paid but little attention to physical sciences, the interests of the Government and of British capital in India obliged them to encourage technological skills in certain limited fields. Thus, the great irrigation projects required engineers. The development of railways under company management required skilled technicians, at least at the lower levels. A few engineering colleges and technical institutions came into being as part of the universities that had already been established in India. But there was no interest in scientific research or learning, and no institutions existed for such specialization. The beginning of the century found India living in an almost pre-scientific age, with but little interest in the advancement of science. The rise of Indian capital, bringing with it the desire to create new industries, made the more far-sighted leaders of India realize the urgency of the problem. Two men deserve special mention in this connection. Jamshedji Tata, a leading industrialist of Bombay, realizing that without advanced scientific research no country can progress, made the first notable endowment which led to the establishment of the Indian Institute of Science in Bangalore (1908). Equally far-sighted was the action of Maharaja Sayaji Rao of Baroda, who established in his own state the first institute of industrial technology. The nationalist agitation in Bengal, following the partition of that province, saw the birth of the Council of National Education which also emphasized the study of modern technology, and the institution which it created for the purpose has now been accorded the status of a university. In the period following the First World War there was a growing demand for scientific and technical education and the universities which came under popular control following the Montagu-Chelmsford reforms of 1919 responded to this growing national need. This period may be said to have witnessed the establishment of scientific work in India. The award of the Nobel Prize to C. V. Raman for his discoveries in physics may well be considered a recognition of India's entry into the field.

Though India had thus a considerable corps of scientists at the beginning of her independence, neither in technology nor in the field of application of science to industry had she made any headway. One of the significant achievements of India, immediately after her independence, was the organization of a network of laboratories for the advancement of research. These institutions fall into three categories : institutions for pure research in science, like the National Physics Laboratory, the National Chemical Laboratory and the Tata Institute of Fundamental Research ; central institutes connected with the application of science to industry, like the fuel research institute, the electro-chemical research institute, the electronic research institute, the metallurgical laboratory and other insti-tutions of a similar nature; and, thirdly, institutions subsidized by the Government of India but financed, mainly, by specific industries to deal with their special problems. The sugar, cotton, textile and jute industries provide notable examples of co-operative research. Their contribution to the industrial progress of the country has been considerable.

Even more significant is the progress that India has made in the matter of atomic research. As early as 1948, India set up an Atomic Energy Commission with the object of developing atomic energy for peace-ful purposes. This must, at the time, have evoked sceptical smiles in the West. It was known that India had a considerable supply of monazite sands and other uranium and thorium-containing material. But did India have the scientific personnel necessary to carry on advanced research, or to apply the results of research to practical purposes? The last ten years have provided the answer. India's first atomic reactor, built by the Atomic Energy Department, went into operation on the 4th August 1956. A new and more powerful reactor is now being erected. Further, the Government of India has now decided to embark on a programme of producing nuclear energy for industrial purposes, and the decision taken is to erect two plants, each generating 250,000 k.w., within the course of the next few years.

The value of the research work carried on under the

Atomic Energy Commission has been recognized by the leading countries of the West, and the progress that India has achieved in this difficult field has helped the outside world to realize that new India is determined not to be left behind in the atomic age.

Apart from the personal interest shown by Mr. Nehru, the credit for this achievement in the field of science belongs to two men—S. S. Bhatnagar and Homi Bhabha. Bhatnagar (who died in 1954) was in many ways a remarkable man. A scientist, trained at Cambridge, his early research work was in the field of chemistry. The contribution he made to the war effort of Britain through scientific work earned him the Fellowship of the Royal Society as well as a knighthood. In the period immediately following independence, he became the champion of scientific work in India, and it was mainly through his efforts that this great chain of national laboratories came to be established in different parts of India.

Dr. Homi Bhabha, the main figure in the field of atomic science in India, comes from a Parsi family, closely connected with the great industrial house of Tata. As Director of the Tata Institute of Fundamental Research, he established early in life his reputation in the field of science. The remarkable progress achieved by India in atomic research has been mainly due to his dynamism and capacity to infuse enthusiasm in younger men. Both Bhatnagar and Bhabha were humanists, with interests outside their own immediate fields of research. Bhatnagar was a poet of distinction in Urdu, while Bhabha is a painter of talent.

Besides the development of higher scientific research, India embarked on a large-scale policy of training technical personnel at all levels. The problem that faced her may be judged from the fact that at the time of her independence Indian engineering institutions produced annually only a modest 940 graduates. Today their number is over 3,000. The total number of qualified engineers in India now is nearly 80,000, but her expanding industries and the major projects of the second and third five-year plans, it is calculated, will require no less than 300,000. As early as 1948, the Government recognized that without a rapid and manifold increase in technical personnel and the creation of institutions for maintaining an ever-increasing supply, her schemes for a planned industrial revolution would not fructify.

The programme that the Government of India decided upon was, first, to expand the existing institutions in the present (second) plan period in order to provide for an additional 2,450 seats for degree and 4,225 seats for diploma courses, thus raising her production of engineers to ten thousand a year. Secondly, the Government planned from the beginning to establish higher institutions for post-graduate and research studies on the model of the Massachusetts Institute of Technology in four major centres of India. The Kharagpur Institute, in the eastern zone, developed mainly with the co-operation of the U.S.A., has already been functioning for over four years. In the western zone, near Bombay, a similar institution with Soviet assistance was established a year ago. In the South, it is with German co-operation that the institute in Madras is to function, while its counterpart in the north will have the support of Great Britain. In another five years India hopes to become self-sufficient in the training of personnel in higher technology.

In addition to this programme of expansion the Government of India has utilized the facilities afforded by the universities and educational institutions of the West and has promoted schemes for the higher training of their technicians in factories abroad. Thus, over three thousand students are undergoing higher education in technical subjects in the United Kingdom, and nearly two thousand in the U.S.A. The Federal German Republic has offered a thousand scholarships a year for study in its institutions. In respect of all such major industrial projects as the new steel plants, provision has been made with the countries co-operating to train higher personnel in their factories. Thus, for the Bhilai steel plant which has been established with the co-operation of the Soviets, over two hundred Indian engineers have received training in higher skills in Soviet factories. Similarly, the British, German and French concerns co-operating with India in various spheres have put into effect schemes for the training of higher technical personnel.

The creation of an adequate technical personnel and the maintenance of a high standard of scientific research are dependent on the quality of general education available in the country. The problem of education in India is indeed stupendous. At the time of her independence, the percentage of literacy in India was

18. The British Government in India had never thought in terms of mass education. When, in the period before the First World War, Mr. Gokhale, the leading Indian statesman of the time, introduced in the legislature a Bill for making primary education free and compulsory, to begin with, in urban areas, it was strenuously resisted by the British Government on the ground of the heavy financial burden involved. The mounting public demand however forced the Government during the Second World War to enquire into this problem and formulate a scheme of national education as a part of the post-war programme of development. The programme then formulated provided for the eradication of illiteracy in India at the end of forty years!

The Indian constitution provides as a directive principle that every child should have the right to free primary education. But though, as an ideal, this is unexceptionable, the problem is complicated by two major factors. The first is the increase in population (amounting to no less than five million a year). Even if India were a fully literate country, the problem of providing facilities for an additional five million a year —trained teachers, buildings, education equipment, etc.—would prove a very difficult one. When to this five million is added the considerable percentage of children of the school-going age who do not today receive education, it will be realized that the provision of universal education, even up to the primary stage, is not easy to solve within the next decade or two.

Secondly, there is also the problem of India's many

languages. One of the fundamental rights of the constitution, enforceable through courts of law, is the
right of a child to be given primary education through
his mother tongue. As the thirteen languages which
are recognized under the constitution are of uneven
development, this creates problems for the education-
ists who have to prepare text-books, provide teachers
and maintain a common standard all over the country.

The immediate question facing Indian leaders is to
decide whether they should concentrate on a high
standard of education for a limited but large enough
section of people, and resort to a programme of
gradualism in the matter of universal education, or
attempt the double task of providing a minimum
education for all and simultaneously undertake a large
expansion of university and technical education. It is
obvious that India's programme of industrial development, as well as her political progress and administrative efficiency, depend on her ability to draw upon a
reasonably large class of highly educated and trained
people. Only when her resources have been greatly
increased as a result of development could the problem
of universal education be satisfactorily solved. It may
also be remembered in this connection that at the time
when the great industrial revolution took place in the
major European countries the problem of universal
education was not even thought of, and it was only
after the enormous increase in wealth which followed
that revolution that even countries like England and
France embarked on a policy of educating the entire
people.

The creation of a large enough educated class on which the progress of a nation depends is the function of universities. At the time of the independence, India had twenty-four universities, three of which (Calcutta, Bombay and Madras) had been established as early as 1857. During the last twelve years, the number of universities has increased to thirty-eight and some of them, like Calcutta and Madras, have many thousand students on their rolls. As early as the second decade of the century, the Sadler Commission on university education in India pointed out that the demand of the middle classes for university education had become a revolutionary fact of far-reaching significance. Today the demand is so great that even the foundation of one additional university a year is unable to cope with it effectively. There are many colleges in India with as many as four thousand students, the teaching work being carried on in shifts as in a factory. The problem of creating a large enough educated class in India presents, therefore, no great difficulty.

The central problem of university education is that of the medium of instruction. Under the system established by Macaulay, the medium of higher education all over India was English, though in the secondary schools, in the later years of British rule, especially after the Montagu-Chelmsford reforms of 1919 when education in the provinces came under popular control, Indian languages had begun to replace English. At the university level, education continued to be entirely through English, except at the Osmania in Hyderabad. This system had, as we have pointed out earlier, certain undoubted advantages, among which should be counted the creation of a progressive intelligentsia having a common outlook, and an understanding and appreciation of the political and social thought of the modern world. It also contributed greatly to the development of Indian languages and, more than all, it gave a sense of unity to the country. But English as the medium of higher education has two major defects which outweigh these undoubted advantages. The extent to which education through English could penetrate was extremely limited. After a century of effort, the British educational system was able to produce less than eight million people with a high-school standard of education in English : in fact, the number of people with an adequate knowledge of the language is considerably less. Secondly, it created a wide gulf between those educated in English and others educated either in the traditional way or through the Indian languages.

It was therefore clear from the beginning that if India was to undertake a programme of national education, it had necessarily to be through the Indian languages. This decision was not merely based on patriotic grounds, but was reached because, from the practical point of view, it was realized that higher education, unless it was given through the regional languages, would inevitably be limited to the upper classes and, moreover, psychologically those languages represented to the people their own cultural inheritance, and were consequently integrated with the national mind.

But that does not mean that English as a language

will become less important in India. In fact, it may become more important, though it will not continue as the sole medium of higher education. What India seeks to do is to encourage the study of English as a *language* at secondary and college levels, especially because it is realized that in the field of scientific work,[1] technology and other essential spheres of higher intellectual activity, India must continue to use English, at least for a considerable time. English will therefore be more than a compulsory second language in the later stages of secondary education and in the universities. Through none of the Indian languages, however developed otherwise, is it possible today to impart higher scientific and technical education, and India is most certainly not likely to deprive herself of the great advantage she possesses of having at her disposal a great modern language through which she can participate in the more advanced developments in these all-important spheres of study.

The problem of a common language for India, though connected with her educational system, has primarily to be considered in relation to national integration. The thirteen languages enumerated by the constitution of India are national languages, and all (except Punjabi and Urdu) cover clearly marked areas and constitute, broadly speaking, the basis of provincial integration. Most of them are highly developed languages—some, like Tamil, having classical literatures of high quality and a history extending over two thousand years. From the point of view of modern

[1] See chapter on education in the author's work on the problems of Afro-Asian States, p. 62.

literary activity, languages like Bengali have reached a level which entitle them to be numbered among the advanced languages of today. There is therefore no question of their being superseded in their own areas or not being encouraged by the central government. In fact, they are already the media of instruction up to university level in many states, and have been recognized at least partially as the language of official work.

But the constitution equally provides that Hindi based on Sanskrit shall in due course be made the official language of the federation, and therefore the medium of communication between the provincial governments *inter se* and between them and the centre, the language of the Supreme Court and legislation and of parliamentary discussions. Hindi, though it cannot claim to be more developed than many of the other languages, is spoken by over 160 million people out of a total of 380 million. Besides, its distribution covers the entire Gangetic Valley outside Bengal (population 110 million), Rajasthan (15 million), Madhya Pradesh, the vast area lying to the south of the Ganges up to, Nagpur (population 25 million), and 7 million in the Punjab. Further, in most of the non-Hindi areas, like Calcutta, Bombay, Hyderabad and in the Andhra cities, Hindi is used as a *lingua franca*. More important is the fact that none of the people of India, except the 100 million who speak the Dravidian language of South India, have any difficulty in mastering Hindi for normal purposes.

So far as South India is concerned, the question of accepting Hindi as the common language, though

complicated, is by no means one of insuperable difficulty. In fact, it has been calculated, that there are no
less than five thousand words in ordinary use which
are common to the languages of South India and to
Hindi based on Sanskrit. The dominance of Muslims
in the north had, during the last three hundred years
introduced into Hindi a large number of Persian and
Arabic words, without however displacing their
Sanskritic equivalents. The emphasis on the Sanskrit
derivation of words in Hindi is not in any sense
designed for the exclusion of Islamic influences, but to
give a greater common background for all the Indian
languages. Already those who know Hindi in the
South number many more than the total English-
speaking population of the whole of India—and this
not merely those who are generally described as the
"educated classes".

It may well be asked why it is necessary to displace
English as the official language, when it has been for
so many years the language of political, and to some
extent intellectual, work throughout India—the language of the courts, of politics and even of religious
thinking. There are many valid reasons which render
such a change unavoidable. If a democratic form of
government has to be successfully worked, especially
on the basis of adult franchise, it is obvious that political
education must penetrate every level of the population.
We have already seen that, after a hundred years of
effort, the British system of education through English
created only a comparatively small intellegentsia,
especially if we take into consideration the size of

India's population. Political power or leadership cannot be confined to that limited class. Already this has become manifest in the way the democratic institutions are working in India. In the central government itself, some of the leading personalities have not been educated in the universities. The late Maulana Abul Kalam Azad, one of the most distinguished leaders of the national movement, who was, till his recent death, one of the most powerful personalities in Mr. Nehru's Cabinet, had only an insufficient knowledge of English : and others, like the Minister of Transport, Jagjivan Ram, had no university education. Among the new leaders who came into prominence after independence, Kamaraj Nadar, Chief Minister of Madras, who has most successfully administered that great province, knows hardly any English. If this is the position in the central and provincial cabinets so soon after independence, it will come as no surprise that in parliaments, assemblies, municipalities, district boards and other representative institutions the English-educated classes cannot continue to maintain their pre-eminence. In fact, "the new people" who are taking over the leadership of the country are more representative of the common people than the English-educated classes who spoke for them in the past. Any attempt to continue English as the language of ordinary higher education, or to uphold its position as the common language of India, would in the circumstances be unrealistic.

It is equally obvious that university education cannot be unrelated to secondary education. Till the Montagu-Chelmsford reforms (1919), the medium of instruction in the secondary schools was also English. Today it is no longer so. Consequently, university education has also, at least in part, to be based on Indian languages.

The educational problems that India faces are therefore extremely complicated. In science and technology she has to keep in line with the most advanced nations ; this requires the continuance of English as a major subject of study, so that India's relations with the modern world in these matters may not in time get weakened. At the same time, she has to evolve a comprehensive system of general education through her own languages. Finally, she has within reasonable time to extend the benefits of education to a population of three hundred and eighty million people, increasing at the rate of five million a year. The magnitude and complexity of this group of problems offer the greatest of all challenges to the leadership in India.

CHAPTER VII

INDIA AND PAKISTAN

THE RELATIONS BETWEEN India and Pakistan are so complicated and govern so many aspects of the policies of the two countries that they require to be carefully analysed and understood before the problems of defence and foreign policy can be discussed. The general idea is that these relations which have become bitter, if not inimical, result from the Kashmir question and from India's attitude towards the waters of the Indus River system. This is far from being the case. The complications about Kashmir and the claims in respect of water are in the main the results, and not the cause, of the deterioration of relations between the two countries, which has a very difficult and often forgotten background.

For over a year before the partition actually took place, the tension between Hindus and Muslims in North India had erupted into an undeclared civil war. Beginning with what has been called the Calcutta Killings, when that great city had been subjected for some days to loot, arson and murder, this state of communal warfare had spread to East Bengal, Bihar, U.P. and the Punjab. It is not possible to allocate blame for this, as communal extremists among both Hindus and Muslims seemed intent on demonstrating their comparative strength. By the time the partition had been effected, the two communities in North India had begun to look upon each other with deep-seated suspicion. There was, however, one major difference. On the Indian side, Mahatma Gandhi, Pandit Nehru and other leaders were actively fighting against such a tendency; while, among the Moslems, though a considerable body of opinion deplored the developments, the Muslim League, perhaps with the intention of demonstrating the inevitability of Pakistan, never raised its voice against this form of civil strife. Thus, when the partition of the sub-continent took place, the sense of fraternity which had, by and large, existed between the two communities had vanished.

Moreover, the first few weeks after partition witnessed an outburst of murderous fury, in which many thousands on either side of the Punjab frontier lost their lives. Again it is difficult to allocate blame. Though this chapter of inhuman cruelty was brought under control after a few weeks, the heritage of bitterness which it left behind on both sides rendered a peaceful solution of outstanding problems between the two countries practically impossible.

In the period immediately following the partition, therefore, popular opinion in both countries developed a feeling of extraordinary hostility, which came to be reflected in the attitude of the two governments and gave even commonplace issues the appearance of intractable controversies.

Apart from the generally hostile atmosphere which vitiated the initial relations between the two countries, there are three continuing factors that have been the cause of much frustration in Pakistan and considerable feeling in India. In combination, they have led to the growth of a psychology of disappointment and anger on the side of Pakistan, and distrust and rigidity on the side of India. In the first place, the leaders of Pakistan had believed that, while their own state would be strongly integrated through its single Islamic ideology, the internal difficulties of India would lead to a breakdown, and perhaps result in chaos. It was freely stated that the princes, to whom Mr. Jinnah had publicly promised non-intervention and even independence if they desired it, would prevent any integration of Indian territory. It was well known that he had promised the former ruler of Jodhpur a guarantee of the state's independence, and free use of the port of Karachi if he did not accede to India. The agreement, which had been practically concluded at the end of July 1947, a fortnight before Indian independence, would have brought Pakistan practically to the doors of Delhi. A group of princes in Central India, led by a Muslim ruler, was encouraged to create a confederation which would give them a corridor to the sea, in order to enable them to ally themselves with Pakistan. Also, it was no secret that the organizations of Muslim extremists in Hyderabad who vetoed every settlement negotiated by the Nizam's advisers were doing so with the encouragement of Pakistan. Mr. Jinnah had thus every reason to hope that India, with nearly half her territory under ruling princes with some of whom (both Hindu and Muslim) he hoped to establish the closest co-operation, would not be able to function effectively or to integrate herself into a state. The result would have been that, while India was weak, Pakistan would be well integrated giving her a dominant position in the sub-continent. When this dream vanished as a result of the patriotism of the Princes and their people, Pakistan found that she was faced with a united India, which separated the two wings of Pakistan by a distance of twelve hundred miles.

A second and equally bitter disappointment was the attitude of the Indian Muslims : the thirty-five million who had elected to remain in India. It should not be forgotten that Pakistan was conceived as the homeland of the Indian Muslims. Its main protagonists had come from Bombay and the United Provinces. But, when the partition came, the vast majority of Muslims outside the provinces which constituted Pakistan elected to remain in India. Pakistan, however, believed that the Muslims of India would at least look to Karachi for protection and support. It was her hope that the Muslims who remained in India would be a source of weakness to the Indian state and would provide her with a claim to intervene in their interest. This calculation again proved to be wrong. The vast majority of the Muslims who remained in India proved not only to be patriotic Indians, but resented the claim of Pakistan to speak for them. Even today, the Pakistani Press is fed with stories of the oppression of Muslims by Hindu India, of the desecration of mosques, injustice to the Muslims in the matter of appointments, and other alleged complaints of this kind. But on every major controversy between India and Pakistan, Indian Muslims have unhesitatingly stood on the side of India. When India was forced to intervene in Hyderabad, there was a widespread feeling in Pakistan that the Muslims in the rest of India would at least create trouble, if not rise in rebellion to support the last vestige of Muslim rule in India. No voice in fact was raised by the Indian Muslims in support of the Nizam's independence. In the Kashmir controversy, again, not only did the Muslim public in India stand solidly behind the Indian government, but Muslim officers of the Indian army were among the first casualties in the struggle. So far as the canal waters are concerned, it is sufficient to note that the Minister in charge of the portfolio today is a Muslim.

How strongly these two factors, the integration of India and the loyalty of Indian Muslims to their mother country, contributed to a sense of frustration in Pakistan may be judged by the fact that Khaliq-u-Zaman, later a successor to Mr. Jinnah as the official leader of the Muslim League, declared in a public speech that the two major dangers to Islam were the establishment of an integrated Indian union of three hundred and fifty million on the one side and the growth of a militant Arab nationalism on the other.

A third source of disappointment was the attitude of the states of the Middle East towards India. Pakistan had hoped that, as the largest Muslim state, with a population almost four times that of Egypt and resources incomparably greater than the countries of the Middle East, she would be accepted as the leader of Islam, which would enable her to isolate India from the countries of Western Asia. During the first two years, many Islamic conferences were convened in Karachi. But here also her policy met with failure. Not only did the other Islamic countries react unfavourably to Pakistan's claim to leadership, but India was able to build up a position of friendship, sympathy and under-standing with the countries of the Middle East, Egypt, Syria, Saudi Arabia, Afghanistan and others.

It is only from this background of disappointment and frustration that the bitterness of Pakistan towards India can be understood. *Khoon se laenge Hindustan* (With blood we shall conquer India) was once the cry, when India seemed threatened with all kinds of troubles. When that appeared totally unrealistic, Paki-stan hit on a new policy of appealing to the world with the cry of a weak state threatened by a larger one in her political and economic interests. It was here that Kashmir and the Indus water claims became important.

The problem of Kashmir, though complicated by many extraneous factors, can be stated in very simple terms. Jammu and Kashmir formed a single Princely State under the sovereignty of the House of Gulab Singh. Like the rest of the Princely States, Kashmir was given the option of acceding either to India or to Pakistan, according to its geographical contiguity. The state was contiguous both to India and to Pakistan and it was open to the Maharaja to join either. But, as the official view of Pakistan at the time was that the princes need not accede to either and could, if they desired, remain outside, the Maharaja hesitated to come to a decision. But Mr. Jinnah, in spite of his public professions, was not prepared to wait. When peaceful pressure failed to achieve the end he had in view, volunteers recruited from the tribal areas in Pakistan began to march into Kashmir looting and plundering the people, with the object of "liberating" the state from Hindu rule.

The justification which Pakistan put forward was that the Maharaja's government was following a policy of ruthless repression in Poonch, a district of the state predominantly populated by the Muslims. In consequence, the population there had rebelled and thrown off their allegiance to the Maharaja. The invasion, it was claimed, was the natural reaction of untamed and fanatical tribesmen against the atrocities practised against their co-religionists. The raiders were from Pakistan, had marched through Pakistan territory and had been supplied with arms from Pakistan arsenals. When the raiders had very nearly reached the capital, Srinagar, the Ruler turned to India for help, and offered to join the Indian union. Thus, legally, as in the case of all other states, Kashmir became a part of India, and the Indian army forced the raiders back from the valley. At this stage, Pakistan's intervention became more open and India, rather than engage in open hostilities, took the case to the Security Council, on the ground of Pakistan's aggression. Through the intervention of the Security Council, a cease-fire between the two parties was brought about, by which Pakistan occupied an area amounting to one-third of the territory. India proposed to finalize the accession by

consulting the people of Jammu and Kashmir when
Pakistan's aggression on Kashmir had been vacated—
that is, after Pakistan had withdrawn her forces from
the third of the state she occupied and had thus recognized the integrity of the state. So far, Pakistan has
refused to do this, and consequently the situation
remains unchanged—India maintaining that Pakistan
has committed aggression against a part of Indian
territory, and is in illegal possession of it, while
Pakistan claims that India is changing the nature of
her relationship with Kashmir, and integrating it with
her own territory without carrying out her promise of a
plebiscite.

What is Pakistan's claim in respect of Kashmir?
Primarily, it is based on the fact that the majority of the
population of the state profess Islam and, as the territory is also contiguous to Pakistan, the conception of a
homeland for Indian Muslims constituted of contiguous
area of Muslim majority would only be partially and
imperfectly realized if Kashmir were to be excluded
from it. The accession of the state to India by the
Maharaja, it is alleged, was brought about "by fraud
and violence" and consequently, it is claimed did not
represent either the interests or the wishes of the people
of Kashmir who had already taken up arms against
him. As India has not given effect to her promise to
consult the people of the state before making the
accession final, it is argued that the present arrangements can only be considered as temporary.

It is also claimed by Pakistan that, strategically,
Kashmir is vital to her, as the possession of that territory

by India would place Pakistan at India's mercy. A third argument often advanced is that the rivers vital to her economy, the Indus, the Jhelum and the Chenab, pass through Kashmir into Pakistan and the possession of the area by India would give her a stranglehold on Pakistan economy. For these reasons Pakistan holds that the possession of Kashmir is essential for her survival.

The argument based on the idea that Pakistan was created as a homeland for Indian Muslims, however fondly cherished by Pakistan leaders, is obviously invalid, as there are in India over 40 million Muslims whose homeland continues to be India. The argument that the accession to India in any case could not be made final without ascertaining the wishes of the people sounds strange when it is remembered that Kashmir has held two general elections based on adult franchise, while in Pakistan itself no general election has yet been held. The argument about the rivers vital to Pakistan economy may appear to have more force. But India has never refused to enter into internationally binding agreements about the use of these rivers. The claim to "the unity of the Indus Valley", like the claim to "the unity of the Nile Valley", cannot over-ride the territorial rights of people.

This, in brief, is the position in respect of Kashmir. For Pakistan it has become a battle-cry—a ground for *jehad*, or holy war against the infidel.

So far as the controversy relating to the Canal Waters is concerned, the situation is also capable of adjustment. The rivers of the Punjab flow from India into Pakistan ;

a very extensive system of irrigation was built up under the British rule which benefits mainly the area now included in Pakistan. There is, however, a very large area in India which in the past has been neglected and, in view of the chronic food deficit from which the country suffers, India is desirous of irrigating this area. This involves no injustice to Pakistan, as there is more than enough water in the Indus river system to meet the requirements of both countries, if proper use is made of the supply available. Over ten years ago India notified Pakistan of her intention to utilize some of the waters of the rivers flowing through her territory to irrigate areas in Eastern Punjab and Rajasthan. At this stage the World Bank intervened and many proposals have been put forward for a systematic use of the waters of the entire Indus river system so that both countries can meet their requirements.

An overall agreement has now been reached as a result of these prolonged negotiations under which by a further development of the waters of the entire Indus river system, with the assistance of Britain, U.S.A., Canada and Australia the interest of both the countries would be adequately safeguarded. This is the first settlement of a major dispute between the two states and may be said to be a turning point in their relations.

Since the eclipse of the political parties, following the establishment of military rule in Pakistan there has been in fact a gradual improvement in the atmosphere of Indo-Pakistan relations. The reasons for this change may be briefly stated here. In the first place the army officers are mostly from the Punjab and the frontier and therefore do not suffer from the same desire to assert their anti-Indian character as the émigrés from the United Provinces and Bombay. Secondly unlike the political leaders who by shouting for *jehad* or holy war as a solution for Indo-Pakistan troubles desired to exploit the popular sentiment, the army leaders, well aware of the dangers of a conflict with India, seem genuinely desirous of settling the outstanding disputes by negotiation. It is yet too early to say whether this change of atmosphere would lead to the establishme nt of a permanently satisfactory relationship between the two countries. But already there is a noticeable improvement in the climate of negotiations. Some of the more important issues are now being discussed with reasonable prospect of early settlement.

There is another problem which, though of diminishing importance, led to deep bitterness at least in the first years after partition. It is the question of the settlement of evacuee property in Pakistan and India. As we noticed earlier, the partition led to a large-scale uprooting of populations on both sides of the Punjab frontier. Though the numbers uprooted from the Indian side of the boundary were perhaps not very significantly less than those who were driven out of West Pakistan, the amount of property involved was altogether disproportionate. While the Muslim population in East Punjab and the western districts of Uttar Pradesh (Gangetic Valley) belonged predominantly to the urban and artisan classes, the Hindus and Sikhs in the Punjab and the Frontier Province contained also a large body of rich traders, industrialists and land-owners. In the prosperous irrigated areas of the Punjab, a disproportionately large area of valuable land was in the hands of the Hindus and Sikhs. Equally in Lahore, Karachi and other West Pakistan cities, the trading and commercial interests, apart from banking and insur-ance, were with the Hindus, who had for long enjoyed a practical monopoly in these lines. When the Hindus and Sikhs were forced out of West Pakistan, they left behind them everything they possessed, just as did Muslims fleeing from East Punjab. The problem of evacuee property was thus a complicated one, and for a number of years was a source of considerable bitterness, especially on the part of Punjabi Hindus, who suddenly saw themselves reduced to utter poverty, through no fault of their own. Equally, on the side of Pakistan, though the assets left by the Hindus and Sikhs more than amply compensated the losses the Muslims suffered by leaving India, the fact that the Pakistan Government has not yet been able to resettle them has added to their frustration and bitterness. So far as India is concerned, though the dispossessed persons from the Punjab have been rehabilitated in India suc-cessfully, and have been a source of great strength to Indian economy, the continuous flow of refugees from East Bengal, which has now reached a figure of nearly three million, has kept alive a bitterness of feeling.

All these factors have produced a deep sense of frustration which has led Pakistan to form strange alliances. The support given by Pakistan to the Portu-guese occupation of Goa is one notable instance. The

Portuguese hold on to their possessions in India, the small territory of Goa and the Isles of Daman and Diu (altogether with a population of 300,000), as if they formed an integral part of Portugal itself. India does not and cannot accept as permanent what is nothing but a historical anachronism. While France willingly negotiated a settlement in respect of its settlements (Pondicherry, Karaikal, Mahe, etc.), the Portuguese have taken up a totally negative attitude, and have inaugurated a policy of open terrorism to keep in chains the people who have been agitating for their liberation. Not even the European allies of Portugal have come out in support of this policy. And yet, as it concerns India, the government of Pakistan has carried her hostility to the extent of openly siding with Portugal and coming to her assistance in every way.

Indian opinion in its turn has become more rigid and generally suspicious of Pakistan politics after many years of experience. The attempt of successive Pakistan governments to utilize the Western alliances, S.E.A.T.O. and the Baghdad Pact, against India, has especially created a reaction in India which has not been helpful towards an understanding. On both sides the climate of opinion has continued to deteriorate.

The future of Indo-Pakistan relations is therefore unpredictable. To any observer it should be obvious that a firm understanding between the two countries would be of the greatest advantage to both. But it is undeniable that, with every change of government in Pakistan, the sentiment against India has become more and more bitter, while India has become more and more suspicious of Pakistan's attitude. If the issues had been merely political or economic, they could have been settled long ago, but since they are psychological, only time and a radical change in circumstances could bring about an understanding. The inescapable fact is that the present generation—leaving aside notable exceptions on both sides—live in a mental atmosphere which is not conducive to settlement. A fairly large section of people in the Gangetic Valley cannot forget that the area now constituting Pakistan was once a part of their motherland. Though they realize that the partition was perhaps inevitable, and could not in any case be changed now, they are still inclined to look upon the people of Pakistan as those who betrayed a sacred cause. In Pakistan, on the other hand, the feeling is almost universal that the partition has worked out unfairly for them. The historic Indian centres of Muslim culture— Delhi, Lucknow, Hyderabad—are not in Pakistan. To the Muslims of this generation, India continues to evoke nostalgia, and it seems a bad dream that their plan of having a dominant voice in India, while keeping their own Islamic homeland, vanished like a mist when the integration of India into a single state was achieved. It should also be remembered that most of the leaders of Pakistan's public life, and the senior members of the civil services, had come into prominence in a United India. Mr. Jinnah, before he took the leadership of the Pakistan movement, had been an All-India leader of the highest standing. Liaquat Ali Khan, the first Prime Minister of Pakistan, belonged to the Karnal Nawabi family in India and his interests were mainly in Uttar

Pradesh. H. S. Suhrawardy and Chundrigar—both Prime Ministers of Pakistan—not only came from India, but had attained high political office in United India. So far as the civil servants are concerned, not only do many of them come from India, but they still have relatives in India. General Mirza belongs to the family of the Nawab of Murshidabad, who are the leading noblemen in Bengal; M. S. A. Baig, the Foreign Secretary in Pakistan, has a brother in the Indian Foreign Service. The instances are so numerous that outsiders find it anomalous and difficult to understand. The cumulative effect of all these factors is that the present generation in Pakistan, while emphasizing the separate nationhood of their country, cannot consider themselves as foreigners in respect of India, and carry on in their politics the struggle with Hindus which brought about the partition. Till a generation grows up in Pakistan which looks upon India not only as a separate country, but as a foreign nation, and which ceases to look upon the Muslims in India as instruments of their policy for whose religious interests they have a responsibility, there seems to be little chance of a better understanding between India and Pakistan, much less of a settlement of their controversies.

CHAPTER VIII

INDIA AND THE WORLD

DURING THE DAYS of the British rule, the Indian
Empire, it had been rightly said, was a continental
system, which extended its influence and authority
from the Arabian coast to Hong Kong. Though a
political structure subordinate to the Government at
Whitehall, the Indian Foreign Office of the British
period initiated and carried out a foreign policy of
which the primary objects were the safeguarding of
India's sea and land frontiers from the encroachment
of any rival European power and the maintenance of the
widespread interests of Britain in Asia. In its relation
to India, this policy led to the creation of a neutralized
area of buffer states around her (Afghanistan, Nepal,
Siam), the establishment of unofficial protectorates over
Sinkiang and Tibet, and the development of special
relations with the Sheikhs and Sultans of the Arabian
coast. This continental system endured till the last days
of British rule. The maintenance of India as the centre
of this system was the primary objective of British
Indian foreign policy.

With the achievement of the independence of India
and the practically simultaneous emergence of the other
Asian states into the international arena, the maintenance of this continental system became impossible, even
if India had had the power or desire to continue it. The

problem that faced new India was to discover and
pursue an alternative policy which, while maintaining
the peace of the area, would also safeguard her interests.
India's foreign policy in regard to the Asian states must
be viewed primarily from this point of view.

i. China and South East Asia

India's position in Asia has three aspects : the
special circumstances arising from the Partition that
govern her relations with Pakistan ; her relations with
China, and her position in regard to Burma, Malaya,
Indonesia, Ceylon and other similarly situated countries. The first has been dealt with separately.

The revolution in China, and the substitution of an
ineffective Kuomintang by the Central People's Republic which exercises undoubted authority over the entire
territory of that ancient empire, is the dominant fact of
Asian history which, together with the independence
and unification of India, gives to the Asian situation its
dynamic characteristics. The relations between these
two countries are particularly important and have considerable influence on other Asian countries.

In history, India and China have, politically speaking, constituted two different worlds which, though
touching on each other, have not influenced each other
greatly. The only problem which existed between them,
which India inherited from the British, related to
Tibet. India, however, recognized Chinese authority
over Tibet and the outstanding issues between the two
countries in this area were settled by negotiations in
1954.

The effective occupation of Tibet by China introduced new and unexpected strains in Sino-Indian
relations. The Tibetans, buried in their mediaeval
monastic traditions, showed themselves intractable to
communist methods. A widespread movement of
resistance which broke out in the country was ruth-
lessly put down by the Chinese. Opinion in India was
deeply moved by the sufferings of the Tibetans, whose
spiritual and temporal Head, the Dalai Lama, sought
and was accorded asylum in India. Indian opinion was
also agitated by the arrival of Chinese troops on the
Indo-Tibetan border. The Himalayan range forms the
natural boundary between India and Tibet. It has
never been, from the earliest times, a live boundary,
requiring elaborate arrangements for defence. Extending from the Pamirs to the Burmese border, over most
of the area, it is settled by long custom and tradition,
but at the North-Eastern end it was defined by
negotiations between the British Indian authorities and
Tibet. This is what is known as the MacMahon line.
China though it had initiated the original agreement
had refused to sign it.

With the arrival of Chinese troops on the Indo-
Tibetan frontier the whole question assumed a new
importance. It became obvious that Sino-Indian relations had now to be defined on the basis of a realistic
appreciation of interests and not on the basis of vague
sympathies. Both parties having realized that boundary
disputes should not be permitted to develop into a
permanent cold war have agreed now that the controversy should be settled by negotiations.

India's relationship with the countries of South and South-East Asia, Ceylon, Burma and Indonesia, stands on a different footing. There is no difference in ideology that interferes in India's relations with these countries. Also, with the single exception of Siam, each of these nations having been under colonial administration has a similar approach to world problems. From the beginning, India has recognized that her policy must be based on the most effective co-operation with these countries, with whose political and economic development her own future is so closely tied. That policy she has consistently followed, eliminating points of difference, enlarging areas of co-operation and working together with them in the sphere of international politics. In fact this forms the nucleus of India's "area of peace"—the group of uncommitted nations which endeavour to keep out of the Cold War and take an independent attitude in world affairs.

It was feared at the time of the withdrawal of Britain that South-East Asia, deprived of the protecting hand of Britain, might become a power vacuum and a cockpit of international rivalry. India's policy in this matter was one of bringing together these states, so that together they could resist any attempts by interested powers to draw them into the whirlpool of the Cold War. Without formal alliances, regional pacts and military groups, India has endeavoured to keep the newly independent states of South and South-East Asia together on the basis of a common policy, the essential elements of which have been : a common support to the peoples subjected to colonial authority in their struggle for

national freedom, a refusal to be allied to one side or the
other in the Cold War, a willingness to co-operate with
all nations for the development of internal resources.
It is her adherence to these principles that has led India
to oppose such alliances as the S.E.A.T.O. and the
Baghdad Pact.

ii.   The Middle East

India's geographical position connects her as much
with the Middle East (Western Asia) as with the
countries of East Asia. Historically, it is significant to
recall that the only serious opposition offered to the
Portuguese domination of the Arabian Sea was when a
combined Indian (Kerala) and Egyptian fleet fought
the Portuguese off Chaul. Again it is necessary to
emphasize that the first adventure of the British Indian
Government in foreign policy was when the Malcolm
mission was sent to Persia to negotiate, if possible, an
alliance with that country against the apprehended
danger of a Franco-Russian attack across the Caspian.
The British Government in India in fact built up a
system of alliances and agreements to safeguard the
Indian and British position on the Arabian coast and
generally in the Middle West. The first treaty with the
rising power of Ibn Saud (in 1915) was negotiated by
the Government of India.

A moment's consideration will show that India is as
much a part of the Middle East as of South-East Asia
or of the Far East. From the earliest times, her trade
was with the ports of the Red Sea and the Persian Gulf.
India, it should also be remembered, has a population

of nearly 40 million Muslims who have traditional relationships with the Islamic world. It is therefore not a matter of any surprise that India should have desired after independence to build up close relations with the countries of the Middle East.

The Middle East countries, most of which attained full independence after the Second World War, have in many ways an approach similar to that of India. Their main interest was to consolidate their independence and to better their economic conditions. But their situation was complicated by the establishment of the state of Israel, which they considered as a permanent barrier to the achievement of Arab unity. Moreover, every Arab country felt that its political independence was limited, either by the rights which the western nations enjoyed by treaty, as in the case of the canal base in Egypt, or by military agreements as in the case of Iraq. Divided into numerous small states, placed in an important strategic position and endowed by nature with immense deposits of oil, these areas became subject to great international pressures as the Western nations, worried by the geographical proximity of the Soviets and their own dependence on Middle East oil, tried to safeguard their position by political and military means. All these factors helped to make the Middle East the epicentre of nationalist troubles during the period.

India viewed the Middle Eastern question from two angles : first, as the final stage of the struggle against the domination of colonial powers, and secondly as an attempt by the Arab people to work out their own destiny without being committed to take sides in the

Cold War. From both these points of view, her sympathies were with the Arabs. Further, being in a sense a Middle East state herself, or, at least, placed between the Middle East and South East Asia, she was also interested to ensure that a powerful new colonialism, however camouflaged, did not develop on her flanks. Out of these factors arose the working programme of the Arab-Asian group in the United Nations, which later found political expression in the Bandung Conference.

India's attitude towards Israel is something which many people find difficult to understand. While India has recognized Israel and co-operates with her in the U.N., she has maintained an attitude of aloofness, which is neither logical nor in conformity with her general policy. For this apparent contradiction there are two explanations: The first is her desire not to alienate her own considerable Muslim population, always sensitive, in matters affecting religion, to the views of Mecca and Cairo, and the second her policy of co-operation with the Arab countries. The possibility of Pakistan seeking to undermine her relations with the countries of the Middle East is a factor which in the present circumstances no Indian statesman could overlook.

iii. India and the Commonwealth

In August 1947, India became an independent Dominion, a member of the Commonwealth, in the same position as Canada and Australia, recognizing the King of England as the constitutional head of the state.

It was understood from the beginning that this was only a transitional arrangement and that, when the constitution was promulgated, she would become a Republic. As Burma had already ceased to belong to the Commonwealth and had become an independent Republic, it was widely believed that India would also cut off her ties with Britain on adopting a republican constitution. But, to the surprise of most people outside Britain and India, the new Republic elected to remain within the Commonwealth, accepting the British sovereign, not as the head of the Indian state, but as the Head of the Commonwealth. To many outside, it seemed that India was still in some sense, British, and that imperial authority, in some camouflaged form, still remained in India. What were India's motives in deciding on this continued association with Britain and her Dominions? Primarily, it was a recognition of the fact that such an association, far from limiting the sovereignty of the new Republic, only helped to strengthen her independence, and to give her a position in the world which individually she could not attain all at once. More than this, the leaders of India recognized that the Commonwealth represented a new type of political association, between peoples whose approach to policies was based on a set of democratic values and practices which, originating in Britain, had been adopted by the member states. As we have emphasized earlier in this volume, new India was heir not only to her own traditions, but to a large extent to the political heritage of Britain, and, in a measure, to the culture of the West. Her political institutions were modelled

largely on those of Britain. Her legal system, except in
the matter of personal laws, was almost exclusively
British. More than all, the new order which her leaders
hoped to build up was thought out generally in Western
terms. Clearly, an association of the kind provided by
the Commonwealth, which, while guaranteeing the
fullest freedom to individual members, afforded them
opportunities of close co-operation, was something
which the leaders of India found attractive.

There were material considerations also which could
not be overlooked. The defence of India had in the
past been the responsibility of Britain. To build up a
modern Indian Army, Navy and Air Force required
the continuing assistance of a major power. As the
organization of the Indian Army was on British lines,
and its training in the past was by British officers, it
was obvious that if the Indian Army had to be built up
as a modern force, it had to be in co-operation with the
British. In the case of the Navy, this was even more
important. The Indian Navy, at the time of independence, was not a force of any great significance. But it
was clear that an independent India, with its long
and unprotected coast-line, would rapidly have to
develop a navy of its own. This required not only the
acquisition of ships, but prolonged training in various
branches of naval activity. Without a close association
with Britain, such a development was impossible for
India in the immediate future. By remaining in the
Commonwealth, India retained not merely British co-
operation in the building up of the Navy, but training
facilities for superior personnel, chances of exercise

with British naval forces, knowledge of the latest technical advances and, in some measure, a share in the great naval tradition of Britain.

These were no doubt important considerations, but what finally persuaded India to remain within the Commonwealth was the recognition of the necessity to affirm its continued co-operation with the Western world. This did not mean being associated with the West in terms of the Cold War. It was a declaration that, in becoming independent, India was not going to forswear the political, social and intellectual traditions which she had developed during her period of association with the West. It was a declaration of faith in parliamentary democracy and in the institutions associated with it, in a social pattern based on equality, justice and liberty, in an economic system which, while guaranteeing freedom, ensured the fullest development of national resources.

Further, the evolution of the Commonwealth as a multi-racial association of states seemed in itself a desirable ideal. Before 1947, the Commonwealth was in effect an association of independent countries of European stock. In 1947, an Act of the British Parliament (The Indian Independence Act) changed its character and transformed it into a multi-racial organization of which three members belonged to Asia. It was after three years of experience as a Dominion that India was called upon to decide for herself whether she would remain as a republic inside the Commonwealth or outside it. If the decision had had to be taken in 1947 itself, there is little doubt that India would have declared for separation. But, by 1950, India had come to realize that the association in no way limited her independence or affected her self-respect, while on the other hand, her membership of the Commonwealth would obviously help to create a better understanding between Asia and Europe. In fact it was realized that the Commonwealth could, in the altered circumstances, become a bridge between peoples of different races.

It was obvious from the beginning that there were conflicting interests within the Commonwealth, that there were major issues on which the member-states felt deeply and were ranged on opposite sides. India was strongly anti-colonialist. Britain was still an Empire with large colonial possessions. Again, the Union of South Africa followed a racial policy which was deeply resented by both India and Pakistan, not only on general grounds, but as stamping the stigma of inferiority on people of Indian and Pakistani origin. Between India and Pakistan there was no friendly feeling. The Commonwealth had its own internal problems, the stresses and strains of which constituted a test for this kind of new relationship.

In the international field, it was always foreseen that the member states would follow their own independent lines. It was on the question of the recognition of the new People's Republic of China that this difference in approach was clearly seen. Britain, India and Pakistan recognized the government of Peking in 1950. Canada, Australia, New Zealand and South Africa continued to recognize Chiang Kai-shek. Then came the war in Korea, in which India took an attitude different from that of Britain and the other members of the Commonwealth. Though this was a major issue of world-wide significance, it led to no crisis within the Commonwealth. In fact it might even be said to have demonstrated the value of the Commonwealth as a political association of nations with a differing approach to problems. Finally came the Middle Eastern issue, the greatest test which the Commonwealth had so far had to undergo, for in this case the members of the Commonwealth were ranged squarely on opposite sides. That it has survived so great a strain is the index of its political vitality. Today India's association with the Commonwealth would appear to be nowhere seriously questioned.

iv. India and the Cold War

India's relations both with the United States and with the Soviet Union have been largely determined by her attitude to the Cold War. The division of the world into two camps, one led by the United States and the other by the U.S.S.R., synchronized with India's appearance on the international stage. With the leaders of both the camps, the relations of the Indian people during their struggle had been cordial. The U.S.A. had been sympathetic to India's claim to independence and had even in the circumstances of war given her valuable moral support. The Soviet attitude towards the liberation of subject peoples had been proclaimed from the earliest days of the revolution, and, though the Communist Party in India played no significant role in the nationalist movement, and had, in fact, aligned itself

with the British during the war, India looked upon the
U.S.S.R. as a friendly country, which was endeavouring
under great handicaps to create a new society within
its own borders. The U.S.S.R. provided an incentive
and an inspiration to those who visualize independence
itself as the beginning of a struggle for a better life
in India.

When the powers of the world ranged themselves in
two opposite camps, India was called on to make a
choice. It was indeed a difficult choice to make. Her
political structure, social ideals and past associations
were largely related to the West. On the other hand,
she could not see the world with Western eyes, nor look
upon Communism as something evil in itself. The
Western conception of the Cold War as a Manichaean
struggle between the powers of Light and Darkness
was something alien to her own philosophy. Good and
evil are mixed in Indian philosophical thought. In fact,
the spirit of India is anti-Manichaean, and therefore
the Western version of the Cold War as a fight between
good and evil seemed to her just another war slogan,
similar to "the war to end war", "war to save civilization", etc.

Nor could India be persuaded that the division of the
world war between the free and the unfree world. That
the great colonial empires should represent themselves
as the free world seemed ironical to Indians, especially
when, in different parts of the globe, these free nations
were engaged in military action to keep others down.
During most of this period, military action on a considerable scale was going on in Indo-China, Algeria,

Malaya and Kenya. No doubt it was claimed that such action was justified in the interests of the people themselves. Yet, for a country which had so recently emerged from its own struggle for independence, the position did not seem so clear, and the claim of the West to represent the free world seemed a little too thin.

Also, Indians could not forget that only quite recently the United States and the other great nations of the West were the allies of Communist Russia and were working in close co-operation to fight Hitler's armies. In India itself, the Communists had allied themselves with the British Government, and it was not that the West did not at that time know what Communism was, or what policy the Communist states were following. That the allies of yesterday had fallen out and were abusing each other did not mean to those who were not partisans that any serious moral issues were involved in the quarrel.

Finally, India, both because of her Gandhian background and her own immediate interest, was wedded to a policy of peace. The Cold War, as Mr. Nehru has never ceased to emphasize, means "thinking all the time in terms of war; in terms of preparation for war and the risk of having the hot war". To India, with social and economic problems of unparalleled magnitude staring her in the face, this constant talk of war and of preparation for war seemed to be suicidal. Apart from all other considerations, the maintenance of a peaceful atmosphere seemed to India to be the first necessity, and consequently, from the very beginning she refused to align herself with either party in the Cold War.

It should not however be understood that India had a greater sympathy towards the Soviet Union than towards the Western alliance. In fact India, while recognizing the right of the Communists to propagate their views, has never tolerated any policy of subversion and has taken a consistently firm attitude in regard to internal intervention by Communists from outside. But there is an essential difference which may be noted. The Soviet actions which have caused the greatest reactions in the Western camp have all been in Europe, and, except in the case of Hungary, are related to the conditions created by the last war. The quarrels over Czechoslovakia, Germany and Austria which intensified the rift between the two camps were exclusively European problems ; they appeared to India not as great moral issues, but as the quarrels of erstwhile allies in the furtherance of their interests. The intervention of the West on the other hand, whether it be in the Chinese Civil War or in Indo-China or the Middle East, appeared primarily as an attempt to maintain colonial authority over Asian nations.

Also, the policy of "containing Communism", when extended to Asia, has taken the form of military alliances and groupings which appear to India as an attempt of the Western nations to re-establish their political supremacy over the weaker nations of Asia. The South-East Asia Treaty Organization, which, it was claimed, was meant to protect the South-East Asian states against Communist penetration, included only Thailand, the Philippines and Pakistan from among the Asian states, while its major partners were the U.S.A., Britain, France, Australia and New Zealand. Again, in the Baghdad Pact, which consists of Britain, Turkey, Iran, Pakistan, and, till recently, Iraq, the military strength is that of Britain. Both these alliances involve the establishment of bases, the supply of arms and equipment, the reorganization of the military forces of the Asian countries concerned, and a close co-ordination of their policies. Whatever justification there might be for these alliances in terms of the Cold War, it is obvious that they mean an effective though disguised revival of the political power of the West over large areas of Asia. To India it looks like a return to colonialism in a new garb, and consequently something which should be resisted.

The system of Western alliances in Asia also brings the Asian countries unnecessarily within the sphere of the Cold War. In the circumstances in which the new Asian countries came into existence, this seems to Indian leaders particularly unfortunate because it diverts their attention from the urgent problems of economic and social development to concentrate on the building up of military power. Nor is it accidental that in the states allied to the West there has so far been but little effort to build up democratic institutions. In fact, from the Indian point of view, the endeavour of the West to extend the Cold War into Asia has been altogether disastrous.

Naturally, India has attempted to counter this movement by building up an "area of peace" consisting of countries which agree to eschew the Cold War psychology and to maintain in regard to world problems an attitude of independent judgment. The principles on which this policy is based have been described as *Pancha Sheel*—co-existence based on equality, non-interference in each other's affairs, promotion of commercial and other interests, etc. This area of peace is not another alliance or political grouping, though the states which subscribe to these principles often follow a common line of policy. Though stigmatized as "neutralism", this policy is essentially different from that of neutrality. All that India, for example, emphasizes is that she is not content to follow other people's judgments on international issues, and will not be committed to partisanship on the basis of alliances and agreements, but must decide her own policy based on her own judgment. Unfortunately, this seems unreasonable to her Western friends, who are convinced of the essential righteousness of their own cause and therefore expect all who are not fellow-travellers to agree with them.

It is of some importance to note that, so far as Asian problems are concerned, there has been no vital area of difference between the Soviets and India. On some of the major issues which interest India, like the fight of subject peoples for national freedom and the struggle against racial inequality, the U.S.S.R. holds the same view as India. As for military pacts in Asia, no doubt for reasons of her own, the U.S.S.R. is as opposed to them as India and the other non-committed countries. Therefore, apart from the fundamental difference between Communism and the principles of Indian political life, there is an area of agreement between the Soviets and India which gives the impression that India's independent policy is more in tune with the policy of the Soviet Union. But the differences are important, even though, as they relate to internal government, they are often overlooked.

These general factors determine to a large extent the relationship of India with the U.S.A. and the U.S.S.R. There is very much more in common, however, between the United States and India than between the U.S.S.R. and India ; in fact, in many respects the relationship between America and India is much more intimate and co-operative. Both have an anti-colonialist background ; both have a democratic approach to problems, a faith in democratic institutions, individual liberty, freedom of the Press, the determination of policies by public discussion, religious tolerance, and faith in people of different racial origins living together—to mention only a few of the ideas they share. Also, basically, in respect of India's economic, social and other development, the U.S.A. has shown a practical sympathy which few other countries have shown. With some of India's major developments like the Community Projects, the U.S.A. is closely associated. India received very valuable assistance from the U.S.A. in the working of the first five-year plan. In respect of the second five-year plan, also, American financial support has been of vital importance.

With so much in common, how is it, then, that on some of the major problems of international relationship

India and the United States seem to be pitted against each other? The primary cause of this difference is India's approach to the idea of the Cold War which she views as not only basically wrong, but as bringing with it into the Asian area the conception of military pacts and groupings. Also, from the point of view of the relationship with Pakistan, these alliances have tended to give the appearance of being directed against India. Though the United States has emphatically repudiated any such intention, the very fact that Pakistan has claimed that her military alliance with America and the re-equipment of her forces through American help would enable her to take a strong line with India has made the people of India feel that the U.S.A., whether she wishes it or not, is being used against India by the leaders of Pakistan. This view gained strength when, on Pakistan's initiative, the S.E.A.T.O. Council discussed the Kashmir issue and passed a resolution on it.

Another issue which helped to create misunderstandings between India and the U.S.A. during most of this time is the position of the Peking Government. In fact it may be said without exaggeration that, from 1950, the question of China has in some ways cast a shadow on Indo-American relations. On the Indian side, there was the feeling that America was unjustly interfering in the Chinese Civil War by the protection and support she was giving to Chiang Kai-shek's government in Formosa, and that, at least in the beginning, the United States was encouraging Chiang to make an effort to return to the mainland. To India, the

Chinese Revolution was till quite recently a major fact
in Asian resurgence, an affirmation of the freedom and
independence of a great people. The Americans, on the
other hand, viewed it mainly as an extension of Communist power which threatened to change the balance
not only in East Asia, but also in the Pacific. American
policy was naturally directed towards a containment of
China by strengthening and guaranteeing Chiang in
Formosa, by support to France in the Indo-Chinese
War (later to the Government of South Vietnam), by
alliance with Thailand, and, finally, by the creation of
the South-East Asia Treaty Organization.

America resented bitterly not only India's champion-
ship of China, but her opposition to these policies,
which attitude seemed to some Americans unrealistic
and to most others pro-Communist. America could not
understand why India did not act to protect Tibet,
though she herself had been an active supporter of
Chinese authority over Tibet so long as that authority
was represented by the Kuomintang. Again it appeared
to American opinion absurd that India, instead of being
suspicious of a Communist China, should work in
friendly relationship with her. This difference of
approach, America looking upon China mainly as an
extension of Communist power, and India till the new
Tibetan crisis looking upon her mainly as representing
the resurgent spirit of Asia, has been one of the main
causes of Indo-American misunderstanding.

But it must be emphasized that these differences do
not touch any fundamental issues ; only the appreciation of current trends. Indo-American relations have

remained fundamentally friendly, though each has been a little surprised and annoyed at the other's attitude and has often vigorously given vent to its feelings. The American Press is often frank and outspoken about India's international attitudes. Frequently it is unsympathetic and even hostile. Not very different is the attitude of the Indian Press, which does not spare American policies in Asia and the Middle East. But to judge from these would be misleading. American assistance to India in her economic plans has been of very considerable importance ; nor has America shown any lack of understanding of India's internal policy, and, as has been said, American co-operation has always been willingly extended in such matters as community projects, public health programmes and educational schemes. Equally, India, in spite of her opposition to such policies as are represented by the South-East Asia Treaty Organization and military support to Pakistan, has shown a full appreciation of the moral qualities of American leadership, especially in the economic field. After twelve years of experience of each other, it may now be stated that both countries have come to understand one another better and have a greater appreciation of each other's point of view.

India's relations with the Soviet Union have not suffered from the same ups and downs, because on both sides there was, after a first period of hesitation, an understanding of the limitations of such a relationship. The Soviet Union realized from the beginning that there was no chance in the immediate future of India turning Communist, and that her leadership was too firmly established for the Communist Party to try any adventurist game. All that the Soviets could hope for, therefore, was that India might not ally herself with the opposite camp. Once the position became clear, as a result of India's attitude during the Korean War, relations became easier, with frequent exchange of delegations, courtesy visits of leaders and assistance from the Soviets for India's scheme of industrialization, notably in the field of technical training and in the establishment of heavy industries.

CHAPTER IX

THE REVIVAL OF CULTURE

THE EMERGENCE OF India as a nation, as we have already seen, was based primarily on a renaissance of Hinduism. But the revival of Hindu religious feeling which is an important and continuing fact in modern India has not had the effect of narrowing her vision, or of limiting her humanism and culture to purely nationalist lines. In fact, the basic reformation of Hinduism as a response to the challenge of the West enabled her to widen her outlook in religious and cultural fields. This became clear from the earliest days of India's independence. The repatriation of Buddhism, which had for over 900 years been practically excluded from the religious tradition of India, showed that the revival of Hinduism was not based on a narrow bigotry. It was the Chakra of Asoka, the great Buddhist Emperor, that new India adopted as her symbol. The encouragement to Buddhist studies, the enshrinement of the relics of Buddhist saints recovered from Britain, the national celebration of the 2,500th anniversary of the Buddha, these, among other facts, should show that the revival of Hinduism *in* has not led to any narrowness of spirit or to a sense of exclusiveness.

Equally, India's attitude to other religions and cultures has been one of active sympathy. Islam, as the *They practice*

religion of forty million Indians, is not only not differentiated against, but active assistance is extended to the
development of Islamic culture. The Aligarh Muslim
University, which is the celebrated centre of Islamic
studies, is a central institution heavily subsidised by the
Government of India. Adequate facilities for the study
of Arabic and Persian exist in most of the universities.
Schools of Islamic theology, like the famous college at
Deoband, receive every encouragement.

The attitude towards Christian missionary activity
is even more significant. It is true that European
missionaries were in the past generally looked upon as
agents of imperialism, the upholders of Western
civilization. Consequently even after independence
there has been some public criticism of their activities,
especially among backward tribes—a survival of the
earlier feeling of suspicion. The Government of India
however has consistently given the missionaries equal
freedom with others to carry on their religious work.
While in most other states of Asia national governments have become associated with religious sentiments (e.g. with Buddhism in Ceylon and Burma,
Islam in Pakistan and Malaya), in India, missionary
work—though deprived of the privileges which it
enjoyed before—is free. In fact, there are more foreign
missionaries working in India today than at any time
in the past. The educational and medical activities of
mission societies have not been interfered with, though,
like all other institutions, they are subject to Government control. It is the conception of India as a multi-
racial state that gives meaning to this attitude towards

different religions. It is also this doctrine which determines her attitude towards the religious and ethnic minorities in India. In the political, administrative and cultural institutions of India, adequate representation is provided for all groups. Thus, in the central and provincial cabinets the minorities are generally well represented. There are at the present time two governors of provinces who are Muslims. A recent Governor of Madras was a Roman Catholic. Some of the most important posts abroad are held by members of the minority communities. The Ambassadors in the U.S.A., Germany and Yugoslavia are Muslims; the Ambassador in Holland is a Catholic; the Ambassador in the Sudan was till recently a Jacobite, a member of the ancient Christian community of Kerala. In the judiciary and the administrative services also, this characteristic of India's composite nationhood is fully maintained.

And the sense of a composite nationalism is reflected in the cultural revival that is being witnessed in India. In art, literature and architecture, the new activity is not nationalist in the narrow sense. The developments in art, while mainly rooted in Indian traditions, derive inspiration equally from movements abroad; from Europe, Mexico and China. It is not a revivalism that India encourages, but a new dynamic activity which rejects nothing which is of value wherever it may come from. So the painting and sculpture of modern India are universal in their approach, and nowhere is the principle better exemplified than in the fields of architecture. In the new cities which India has constructed after independence there has been no attempt to go back to a purely Indian style. What India has sought to do is not to revive the glories of Taj Mahal or the Ellora temples, or the magnificent architecture of the Orissan or South Indian temples, but to create a new style suited to modern conditions. The new city of Chandigarh, built at the foot of the Himalayas, designed by the French architect Le Corbusier, is the symbol of India's new architecture. In the new capital city of Bhubaneswar in Orissa, though a much greater emphasis is laid on local architectural features, the broad line of a new synthesis has been maintained. In fact it can be said that, for the first time since the eighteenth century, India is now developing a new architecture.

In literature, also, the dominant tendency after independence has been to approximate more closely to modern forms and techniques. This has manifested itself in all Indian languages side by side with a great revival of Sanskrit and Pali and other classical studies. The importance attached to Sanskrit in modern India as the source and inspiration of Indian literatures and the revival of Sanskrit studies all over the country are evidences of the emphasis that India lays on its own cultural traditions. But equally significant is the fact that the creative activity in modern Indian languages is dominated by new ideas and new forms, mainly based on the modern literatures of the West.

The Government of India has attempted to encourage and guide these tendencies by organizing autonomous national academies covering the entire field of cultural activity. The three central academies, Letters, Art, and Music and Drama, constituted on an all-India basis, seek to ensure standards and to develop all-India appreciation of regional activities. The states have also been encouraged to establish local academies on the central model. One of the first decisions of the national Academy of Letters was to bring out under its auspices translations into Indian languages of the best books from foreign literatures, Greek, Latin, Arabic, Chinese and Japanese, as well as the languages of the West. The Academy of Fine Arts seeks not only to encourage modern art, but to popularize among the common people the artistic traditions of India.

In India more than in most countries, national culture had been the monopoly of the higher classes. During the last hundred and fifty years, when in the now advanced countries culture began to penetrate to the masses, in India the system of education through English which the British Government introduced had the effect of producing only a limited intelligentsia, who were themselves, at least till the beginning of the century, cut off from the masses. Also, the early years of English education led to a depreciation of Indian artistic tradition. It was the dogma of the English educators of the nineteenth century that all genuine art originated in Greece, and that Indian art was no more than a curiosity. To some extent educated Indians had become strangers to their own traditions in painting music and sculpture. It was only with the national revival that these classes came to know something of their own inheritance, and the question of taking this culture to the masses did not naturally arise during the period of British rule. The primary endeavour of independent India has been to make the masses of people share in India's culture.

The reorganization of rural life, through Community Projects and National Extension Schemes, provided a machinery for this purpose. With the assistance of radio and the cinema, it was possible to penetrate the rural communities to an extent that had not been possible in the past. Community radio services are an important feature of the programme of rural re-organization and though, owing to the limited supply of electric power in the villages, its influence has so far not been very extensive, it is a growing factor whose significance cannot be overlooked. The cinema has been a much more powerful medium in the projection of culture in India's villages. India has the second largest film making industry in the world—next only to Japan —and it penetrates every part of the country. Its influence in bringing home to the rural areas the cultural inheritance of India was recognized early by the Government, and it is today one of the most important factors not only for bringing to the common man in the rural areas his own cultural inheritance, but in empha-sizing India's cultural unity.

What India has so far done has been to lay the foundations for a revival of culture, and to extend its influence to the masses, to base this revival firmly on national traditions, while welcoming influence from all sources.

CHAPTER X

SOME TRENDS

AT THE END OF twelve years, India has some notable achievements to her credit. She has created and worked with success a democratic system of government. She has reorganized the structure of the State, maintained an efficient administration and built up a body of competent personnel for handling the expanding industrial and political activities of government. These are no mean achievements for a country of the size, population and administrative complexities of India. She has carried through successfully her first five-year plan, laying the foundations of large-scale industrialization, and developing at the same time her agricultural resources and successfully overcoming a menacing shortage of food grains. A planned transformation of rural life has been undertaken under a system of Community Projects and National Extension Services. Far-reaching social changes have been introduced, modifying the family life and inherited customs of the Hindus, abolishing untouchability, undermining caste, breaking up the joint family—in short, laying the foundation of a new Hindu society. All this has been achieved by the normal democratic processes of public debate and discussion, and in an atmosphere of peace.

These are undoubtedly to the credit of the new state. As against these, we may now consider the more obvious weaknesses and dangers that face India.

In the field of politics, a democracy based on a largely illiterate and uneducated electorate has obvious perils. Over sixty per cent of the voters in India can neither read nor write, and, spread over the country, there are backward communities whose situation is no doubt improving but who have not by any standard reached a level of life which enables them to use the political power entrusted to them. While these are no doubt diminishing factors, and, if the present rate of advance could be maintained, would become unimportant in the course of a few years, as matters stand, the danger from an uneducated electorate is a fairly serious one. This is not apparent today, because India's leadership is something inherited from the revolutionary period and has therefore unusual prestige and authority. Also, broadly, it represents national interests. The electorate knows and trusts Mr. Nehru and his close associates as those who fought for and won their freedom. But once the magic of their names ceases to be potent, one of two things might easily happen. Demagogues might sway the electorate with utopian proposals, and establish a reactionary régime, playing on the religious and communal feeling of the populace which could easily be roused. Fear of Pakistan could be worked up, and defence of religion could become a cry as much in India as in Pakistan. In the period immediately following the partition there was a demonstration of this possibility when the R.S.S., a militant Hindu organization, carried on a vigorous propaganda for the Hinduization of the State, and found considerable support for it. The Mahatma had to pay with his life before the public of India could be awakened to the danger to her free institutions which this movement involved; and it is by no means an assured fact that the same dangers will not rear their head again if the central leadership of India weakens, or if the Congress party, which for historical reasons has today an all-India authority, splits up into factions or loses its hold on the masses.

The danger is all the greater because of the federal structure of the government which encourages the development of leadership on a provincial basis. It was the fight against the British Government that developed an all-India leadership in the country, but even at the height of the nationalist movement the authority of the leaders—except Mahatma Gandhi and Mr. Nehru—was based on their influence in their own provinces. Even such men as C. R. Das and Vallabhbhai Patel drew their main sources of strength from their own provinces. That was to a large extent unavoidable. In the future however, when, as a result of the federal structure of government, effective administration will be more and more concentrated in the provinces—in themselves large units, comparable in size and population to major European countries—leadership will tend to become increasingly provincial. Normally there should be no danger in this development. In fact it may prove the best and most effective barrier to military coups d'état such as have taken place in other Asian countries, But the opposite danger of provincial leadership becoming either revolutionary, and in a measure at variance with the centre (as has recently happened in Kerala), or reactionary (as very nearly happened in the state of Orissa), cannot be overlooked. This is an unavoidable feature in a federation as the recent conflict between President Eisenhower and Governor Faubus has proved even in America. In India it has a special significance, as the integration of the Indian people is in some ways incomplete. But it would be an exaggeration of the evil to see in the development of regional feeling a threat to India's unity. The claim of different groups to separate statehood, and the conflicts arising therefrom (e.g. the controversy between the Mahrattas and Gujeratis in the combined state of Bombay), are undoubtedly important as emphasizing this feeling of regional particularism. But such conflicts in themselves do not necessarily contain the seeds of disruption.

The danger of social reaction is much more important. It is often said that India is a museum of all civilizations; that together with an increasing body of atomic scientists and the most modern minded men there exist primitive communities which have not mastered elementary techniques; that side by side with the most advanced ideas are found such things as the fervent worship of cows, and faith in astrology and in antiquated systems of medicine. That in an ancient country with a continuous civilization such survivals of primitive ideas should be in evidence, and should be cherished by the ignorant, is not surprising. Indeed, it is not an unfamiliar phenomenon, even in the most advanced societies. What is surprising in India is the prevalence of these things among large numbers of people who enjoy power, prestige and authority. Besides, and more significantly, many of these beliefs are not held privately as in other countries, but often form part of political programmes and public activities. To take only two examples : the Hindu community, generally speaking, considers the cow to be a sacred animal. Whether there is any religious authority for such a belief is not certain. Indeed, it has been held by scholars that the killing of cows for purposes of food was quite common among Hindus in historic times and that there is no religious sanction for the sacredness which is now generally attached to them. Be that as it may. The strange thing in India today is the vociferous demand of many sections that cow-killing should be prohibited by law. Though pseudo-economic arguments are often advanced in support of this demand, it is well known that the purpose is to exploit the superstitions of the masses to attain political authority.

Nothing shows so much the contradictions in Indian life as this artificial agitation. Everyone who has given any serious thought to the question is convinced that the prohibition of cow-slaughter would be disastrous to Indian economy, but, for fear of alienating public opinion, even the Communists have not taken up the problem of eliminating unnecessary cattle. Consequently, the cow remains sacred even in the present atomic age.

A second example of the strength of social reaction is the agitation in favour of the traditional system of medicine, to support which many provincial governments spend considerable sums of money. The central

government is also under constant pressure to encourage the indigenous systems of medicine which are
vaguely considered as national. It is undoubtedly true
that India was one of the pioneers of medical science in
ancient days, and the Hindu system known as *Ayurveda*
spread practically all over Asia before the tenth century
A.D. It is also true that many of the drugs used by the
practitioners of Indian medicine are efficacious—
indeed they are being regularly incorporated into the
world's materia medica : those facts, however, do not
constitute a scientific system of medicine. Yet every
provincial government is supporting *Ayurvedic* schools
for the teaching of this antiquated system, which is
somehow identified with the national greatness of
India.

These two instances, among many which could be
adduced, would prove that reaction, though in retreat,
is well entrenched in the minds of the masses, and it
will take many years of hard work, under enlightened
leadership, before the danger of at least a temporary
reversion is altogether eliminated. If there is any
weakening of central leadership, then it is obvious that
these tendencies may become stronger. No doubt such
a change would only be of a temporary character,
because, with the changing economy and the transformation now taking place in rural areas, the chances
of a permanent reversion to orthodoxy are indeed
remote.

Another tendency which has manifested itself in the
new society of India during the last twelve years is the
weakening of the middle classes, the classes which

previously provided political leadership and administrative personnel. India has opted for a socialist pattern of society, and the system of taxation which it has accepted presses heavily on the middle classes. In a society where the working classes are educated and trained to public life, such a weakening of the middle classes may not be harmful to society in general. But in India the position is different. Leadership in most spheres of life—political, economic, social and cultural—must for at least a considerable time more come from the middle classes. With a vast illiterate population no other choice is open to India. But the taxation policy of the Government, whether based on a theoretical faith in the doctrine of economic equality, or forced by the necessity of finding money for its large schemes of development, is undoubtedly impoverishing the middle classes to such an extent that it may weaken' the leadership necessary both in politics ànd in administration.

There are many other tendencies which are apparent even to a casual observer, such as the control of the organs of public opinion by industrialists and financiers; the growing gulf between the rural and urban population; the problem of the growth of population and its pressure on food production.

This last question, the steady growth of population, constitutes the most important problem facing the future of India. An increase of sixty million in the next decade will make the population of India around four hundred and fifty million. In twenty years it will have passed the five hundred million mark—a factor of tremendous explosive capacity, whose significance cannot be discussed here. The Government of India, aware of the menacing implications, has embarked on a policy of national family planning. It is not yet possible to say how far such a policy will be successful in overcoming the inherited prejudices, religious sentiments and general immobility of mass opinion.

Most of the tendencies briefly analysed here are not peculiar to India, but apply equally to other democracies. In India, because democratic institutions are new and are based on a largely illiterate electorate, they have a special significance that cannot be underestimated ; but, in comparison with tendencies in favour of progress, and of a steady evolution to a self-developing economy and a modernization of social and political life, they will be seen to be of diminishing importance. The dynamism of India's revolution has by no means weakened. If it were to show a tendency to slow down or to be misled, the developments in other countries in Asia provide her with sufficient incentive to greater effort. The gigantic experiments in revolutionary China, no less than the growth of military dictatorship in many Asian countries as a result of the failure of this dynamism, are factors of major importance in the political psychology of India. India has therefore every reason to continue to move forward with vigour in the path she has chosen for herself, and the trends that indicate weaknesses in her society are but the survival of ancient problems which she has set herself to remedy.

CHAPTER XI

CONCLUSION

IT WILL BE SEEN from the brief analysis in the fore-
going chapters that it is a comprehensive revolution
that has been taking place in India since independence.
It has three major aspects : the transformation of an
ancient society, radically changing its age-long institutions, abolishing untouchability, uprooting caste and
re-ordering family life ; a rapid and planned development of its economy by the introduction of new
techniques and skills and by large-scale industrialization, based on a new scientific outlook ; the reorganization of the rural life of India, breaking down its
inherited and deep-rooted system of village communities and replacing it by larger, economically
self-sufficient units. These three aspects are inter-
related and, though each by itself constitutes a
revolution of no mean significance, cumulatively they
stand out among the landmarks of modern times. The
emergence of India as a modern nation is not so much
due to the political independence of the country, as to
the peaceful transformation she has been able to effect
in a comparatively short time, integrating into a single
whole a population of nearly four hundred million
people, and ensuring its evolution as a dynamic and
progressive force in the world.

It is India's democracy that has provided the impulse

for this continuing revolution. It is the political power
of the masses that enforces these changes and ensures
their continuity. The conservative elements which, as
everywhere else, sing the glories of the past and desire
the maintenance of the *status quo* find that, faced with
the desire of the masses, they are helpless to prevent
these changes or even to slow down the process. This
was convincingly proved in the case of the social
legislation which we have alluded to earlier. In the
provisional Parliament of India legislation had been
introduced, then known as the Hindu Code Bill, meant
to give effect to important changes in Hindu law.
Opposition among the conservative sections of the
Congress argued that, in the absence of an express
mandate from the country, so radical a reform should
not be passed, especially by a provisional Parliament
which had been elected for the purpose of drafting a
constitution. Mr. Nehru accepted this challenge and
made the reformation of Hindu law one of the major
planks of his election platform. The conservative
opposition—especially the Hindu Maha Sabha, which
had taken a definite stand against such legislation—
was practically wiped out in the elections that followed.

New India is based on a conception of life which
does not belong to the West, nor wholly to her own
past traditions. She calls her new economy "Socialism",
but defines it as something which has grown out of
Indian roots and has been shaped by India's needs. It
does not trace its parentage to Marx, Lenin or the
Fabian Society, and yet, as we noticed in its planning,
it has been influenced by Marx and Lenin, and in its

programme by the Fabians. All the same, its ideal remains characteristically Indian, emphasizing the importance of a dispersed economy and the integration of social life in the rural areas, and devoting primary attention to agriculture. Class war is no part of the theory of Indian socialism. Equally, in her social legislation, India does not attempt to imitate the West. It is an Indian society that she seeks to rebuild with the help of modern ideas.

Nevertheless it should be repeated that, though her developments are related to her own requirements, India has freely borrowed from the West many ideas which she has assimilated to her own tradition. She has never, in three thousand years of history, hesitated to take from others what she considered to be of value. A century of close association with the West enabled her to share in the political, legal and social ideas which were then developing in Europe, and, at a later period, to assimilate the new scientific thought which had helped to transform Europe. Thus the life that India is developing is a new life, a synthesis, though no doubt imperfect, between the East and the West. This is the paramount significance of the great experiment now being carried on in India—that it is an attempt to develop four hundred million people, a sixth of humanity, along an independent and distinctive life of progress.

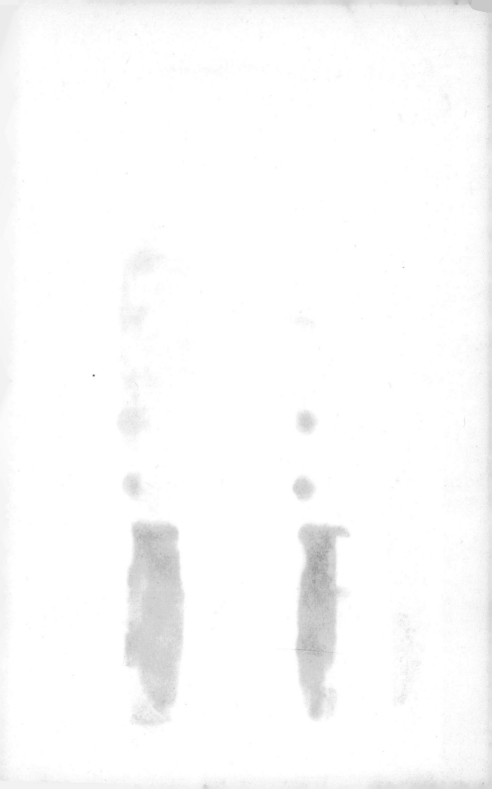